T0147165

What People are Saying about "Jill's Journey"

"This heartfelt journey radiates with positive energy and genuine emotion. It is a beautifully written book that will help so many people. We are all on a journey of our own. This book will inspire the possibility that there is always more than one approach to health, wellness and balance in your life."

— Andrea Wilsdon

"As a broadcast journalist, I've interviewed many authors about their books. Jill's Journey is different. It is uncommonly real, honest and emotionally expressive on a human level we can all relate to. While Jill shares her deepest fears, confusion and disappointments during an intense battle with cancer, she also celebrates her ultimate triumphs and faith in the power of positivity and the mind/body connection. Jill's courage and determination to own her destiny and take full responsibility for her choices offers a roadmap to others embarking on the same path and sends a message of hope and inspiration to anyone experiencing challenging times. Jill's Journey is a good news story!"

— Connie Smith,
Former News Anchor
Order of Ontario
www.conniesmith.ca

"Jill has the ability to turn around any situation and make it positive, to see a solution to every problem. Jill's strength is her desire to help others. She is a born communicator, the strongest, most determined lady I know. Having read 'Jill's Journey', I am no longer afraid of Cancer. I take with me her teachings regarding Positive Thought, the importance of looking after our bodies, emotionally and nutritionally. Her journey is a fascinating insight of pain and fear, laughter and tears, love and determination, and peaceful acceptance that everything happens for a reason."

— Debbie Hutcheson

"Jill's Journey will be helpful for anyone dealing with health issues – not only a cancer diagnosis. I especially like the suggestion regarding making twenty cards to describe goals or hopes for your life. It is a handbook of self-care, determination, and a lesson in loving oneself! Jill is a wonderful woman that

I have been privileged to call my friend for over ten years! Her strength and support for others is her greatest asset. Jill's Journey is an amazing, insightful look at her journey through a cancer diagnosis. She openly shares with the reader her fears, her emotions and her choices. Through all this, it is very obvious how strong and committed she is to healing herself. A great book!"

— Fran Hoppa,
Retired Pharmacist

"Thank you, Jill, for having the courage to share such a tumultuous, trying and expansive time in your life. Your story reminds me of the power of the human heart and mind, and how important it is to invest the time to take care of ourselves BEFORE we get sick, and how to change our relationship with illness and how a new perspective can impact your road to recovery."

— Jennifer Lyall,
Spiritual Mentor and Intuitive Teacher

"Jill arrived in my life by 'coincidence' not long before her life path was to take an unexpected detour down a road less travelled. 'Jill's Journey' is the true story of a tenacious, spirited woman's journey from the diagnosis of a potentially life threatening and overwhelming disease to embracing her new life with the insights she gathers. This book is for those ready to consider options beyond the 'conventional only' approach in addressing a diagnosis of dis-ease. 'Jill's Journey' is just that - an inspiring journey filled with the wisdom, resources, celebration of spirit and messages for life. Jill discovers there are choices available to her and all that is possible as she transitions during a two year period against all odds, despite the suggestion of a severely limited life expectancy. Spend a few hours with Jill as she discovers a whole new world of possibilities and shares the journey of 'her truth' with the world. We can't help but have our curiosity sparked as we journey along side this beautiful soul and experience life shifts and transitions with her."

— Simone Usselman-Tod,
Former Registered Medical Radiation Technologist;
Main care giver of late husband diagnosed with cancer;
Health and Wellness Practitioner

"I have read this book through and through and what an amazing story! Jill's Journey is not only for people enduring health issues, but for anyone to consider for making positive changes in their overall wellness. Some people diagnosed with a disease choose to enlist a naturopath and it amazes me that the first item of business is a change in lifestyle. This change includes focus on the mind, body and spirit - not just the disease itself. Jill's book takes a look at just that and how making these types of changes may help tremendously with surviving such a diagnosis and living life well again. I so appreciate where Jill has been and what she has gone through although I would prefer to avoid it if I could. Her amazing journey inspires me to begin my *own* changes to a healthier me. Thanks to Jill for sharing her story."

— Sandi Holst
Business Instructor

"Jill's Journey is a thought-provoking and practical book that illuminates complimentary approaches to Western medical treatment for breast cancer. Jill's ability to speak from the heart in her recounting of her personal two-year victorious journey with cancer is both heartrending and inspirational. A must read for those looking for clarity in the myriad of options available while going through cancer treatment."

— Barb Leese, MA, Eryt, RYS
Yoga Instructor/Yoga Training Teacher

"Not only was this a story about one woman's journey from a cancer diagnosis to recovery, Jill offered me resources that not only helped her at her time of need, but can help anyone of us improve and attain a higher quality of life - physically, mentally and spiritually. I found this book to be an indispensable resource and an inspiring and uplifting story of Jill's journey and her many choices to healing. Thank you to Jill."

— Deborah Ferdinand
Creative Consulting Services
(289) 969-9287
http://www.creativeconsultingservices.ca

Jill's Journey

EMBRACING MEDICAL & HOLISTIC CHOICES TO HEALING

JILL ROBINSON

BALBOA.
PRESS

A DIVISION OF HAY HOUSE

Balboa Press books may be ordered through booksellers or by contacting:

Balboa Press
A Division of Hay House
1663 Liberty Drive
Bloomington, IN 47403
www.balboapress.com
1 (877) 407-4847

Because of the dynamic nature of the Internet, any web addresses or links contained in this book may have changed since publication and may no longer be valid. The views expressed in this work are solely those of the author and do not necessarily reflect the views of the publisher, and the publisher hereby disclaims any responsibility for them.

The author of this book does not dispense medical advice or prescribe the use of any technique as a form of treatment for physical, emotional, or medical problems without the advice of a physician, either directly or indirectly. The intent of the author is only to offer information of a general nature to help you in your quest for emotional and spiritual well-being. In the event you use any of the information in this book for yourself, which is your constitutional right, the author and the publisher assume no responsibility for your actions.

Editor: Herb Holst
Author photo provided by: Sandi Holst

Print information available on the last page.

ISBN: 978-1-5043-5569-8 (sc)
ISBN: 978-1-5043-5571-1 (hc)
ISBN: 978-1-5043-5570-4 (e)

Library of Congress Control Number: 2016906420

Balboa Press rev. date: 5/16/2016

To those I love and I have loved
…until we meet again.

Contents

"With everything that has happened to you, you can either feel sorry for yourself, or treat what has happened as a gift. Everything is either an opportunity to grow or an obstacle to keep you from growing. You get to choose."

— Dr. Wayne Dyer

Preface

To this day, I honestly can't tell you exactly why I am still living on planet earth since my breast cancer diagnosis two years ago. What I **can** tell you is that it has completely changed my life. I did almost every medical/conventional option that was offered to me along the way, and I embraced more holistic/complementary therapies and options than any other person I have talked to thus far. It was far from an easy path and the decisions I had to make were often times…. daunting. I have learned that my choices were vastly different from those of many others!

So, why **am** I still here? Was it the chemotherapy? The radiation? The surgery? The holistic remedies and treatments I embraced and am still taking to this day? Was it the diet change and taking even more responsibility for my body and health? Was it the meditation? Praying? Visualization? Affirmations? Was it my mindset and brutal determination to stay alive as long as I can in this world? Or was it a combination of **all** of them? This is something I may never know.

Wouldn't it be amazing if I could travel back in a time machine, and try taking away or changing my choices to see if the outcome would be the same or different? Obviously, this is not an option.

What I **have** realized is there is a common thread that goes through what I call "My Journey" which will be shared with you. Whether you have been recently diagnosed with cancer, whether you have other health issues, or you just want to be "healthier", the answers for getting better may be in these pages. The answers, and this may sound strange to you right now, are within yourself. It comes down to choices!

When you or someone you love is diagnosed with cancer, you can be inundated with hundreds of opinions…opinions from people who are expressing it out of concern and love; people who are handling the news in their own personal way; people that just want to help and give their experiences.

If you choose to go the "online" route, be prepared to see literally thousands of options from medical/conventional, to holistic/complementary, and also spiritual options, including limitless different beliefs. It's all out there. It's all available for you at the click of a button, to read and question "is this going to help me and who should I trust?" It can be overwhelming to say the very least.

I hope that by sharing my experience, this book will benefit, comfort and strengthen anyone who may be going through a difficult prognosis or time in their life. The book is written to share my journey, but more importantly, to help you find your way through your own journey. Your journey doesn't necessarily have to be one that includes cancer. This book is intended to help you regardless of what health issues or conditions you may have. I have written it in a way that will hopefully help on all levels: physically, emotionally, mentally and spiritually.

My hope, as well, is that this book will illustrate that there **are** options out there…many options indeed. It is my passion that whatever it is that has put this book in your hands, it will help you and give you hope and energy to move forward to make your life better! Hope is a very powerful word and sometimes that's all a person needs to move forward in their life whether that means recovering from illness or finding a healthier life.

What you will find through reading this book is that one of the most important things you can do is trust yourself in the choices you make. There is no right or wrong in any decision you make in your life. You can gather the information and then see what resonates with you. You will be getting many opinions from different people who have either been through a similar journey themselves, or know somebody who has been through it. There will be people who care about you so much that they just want to help you because they love you so much and because they are literally desperate to keep you on the planet.

The bottom line is that whatever you choose is **your** choice and nobody else's. I want to point out that regardless of whether we live for another day or until we're 101, we actually live each and every moment of our days with **ourselves.** We obviously will spend moments with family, friends, co-workers, total strangers and the like, but the bottom line is that, in the end, every moment always includes **ourselves.** It's very important to be at peace with the decisions that you make.

I hope you are able to enjoy the ride to self discovery through these pages. Perhaps enjoy finding the answers to questions you may have about what to do next. Most of all, enjoy your moments day-to-day and trust yourself to do what is best….for you.

Please join me on "My Journey" and may it help and inspire you on yours - whatever that may be or wherever it may lead you.

"No one saves us but ourselves.
No one can and no one may.
We ourselves must walk the path."

— Buddha

Introduction

January 27, 2014... a day I will never forget...a day that is seared into my memory; the day I received the type of news that most of us have nightmares about; the day that began what I call "My Journey". That day, which easily could have been labeled "My Fateful Day", was the day I received a call at four o'clock from my general practitioner medical doctor telling me that the biopsies taken on my right breast showed up with three areas of cancer, "ductal carcinoma" to be exact, or cancer in the milk ducts.

You might as well have told me that I was Santa Claus in that moment for the disbelief I felt. It came to me as an intense shock as it did for everybody else in my life. *This can't be happening. After all, I was the person that was so healthy and looked after myself and exercised and always ate the right things. I was so positive and holistic! How could this be?* I just remember being so stunned. I was questioning everything in myself and my life and thinking: *Why me? This has to be a mistake or a very bad dream!*

My memory definitely has its moments of vacancy, but at that four o'clock moment I can actually remember <u>exactly</u> where I was in my house when I received that call. I was on my own at the time and heard the phone ring. *Just go answer the phone, Jill... and don't forget to check the 'call display'. I'm not in the mood for a sales call for carpet cleaning or chimney sweeping!* I saw the caller ID and it said the name of my doctor's office. My heart sank in my chest. *This was "the" call I was waiting for. This was the moment of truth when I will find out the results of the biopsy of my breast lump from six days ago!* When I heard my doctor's voice, my heart sank down even further. *She never calls me. I've been a patient of hers for more than 17 years. Why isn't the nurse calling? Why is SHE calling?* I paced around the basement, waiting with my breath almost stopped. She gently delivered the news to me. The serious voice came through the phone with the news. *Did I just hear that correctly? The pathology came back and I DO have breast cancer? Wait, what?* She said she was sorry to have to call but wanted me to know as soon as possible. Her voice started to fade into the distance as my head started to spin. She then asked me "Are you alone at the moment? Are you okay Jill?" As I mentioned, I remember exactly where I was in the basement at the time.

Standing still and after saying goodbye to her, I pressed "end" on the phone. My head was spinning. *What? What? That can't be right! Really? Seriously? How could this be?* I immediately went for a walk in the cold, winter-covered forest with my dog, PT, feeling complete shock and disbelief. As I walked along the Bruce Trail, I ran my doctor's voice and words in my mind over again and again. *Is this a dream? Is this really happening? Who do I tell? What do I do now? How did this happen?* I kicked through the newly fallen snow like it was to blame. I yelled loudly at the sky and the trees as I walked along. I cried. I laughed hysterically. Despite my frantic, frustrated outbursts, trotting alongside me was my furry companion, unaware of anything but where the next best sniff will be and where are those squirrels hiding anyway?

When I got back to the house an hour later, quite honestly, I wanted to go under a rock and just stay there. I just wanted to make the whole world and my new reality go away. In fact, that is exactly what I did for almost 24 hours. I told my husband, Steve, the news from the doctor when he got home from work. I saw the terror in his eyes. *Oh God…this is really happening. It's **not** a dream.* I thought: *I just won't talk to anybody else. I won't tell anybody and I'll just go in my bed and stay there forever. Stupid life anyway! What the hell? After all, I'm the one who has been into complementary and holistic therapies for such a long time! I even have my own business offering my clients holistic healthcare for the last 20 years. I have helped so many people! Was that all just a farce?!*

I dragged myself upstairs to my personal sanctuary - my bedroom - and found some form of refuge under the covers in my bed. As I lay there motionless under the mountain of covers in the stark, intense darkness, I fully believed that the world might just actually go away. I cried until there were no more tears left. I felt intense anger. I felt confused. I had lost many loved ones from cancer – my mother, my dog, and dear friends, but the grief I felt was like nothing I've never experienced before. I was grieving the loss of my life as I knew it. I was in total disbelief and I was frustrated. I didn't want to talk to ANYBODY. *Maybe if I stay here, I will wake up from this nightmare and it will all go back to the way it used to be! Maybe it will just all go away.*

To say Steve was very concerned about me is a huge understatement. At the time, I was completely blind to what **he** must have been going through with the news of my condition. Here was his wife that he loves so much, his best friend for whom he would do anything. He must have thought to himself that this can't be happening! So, as thoughtful and sweet and amazing as only he can be, he called my friend Lesley over to help me. Lesley is a psychotherapist but has also done shaman work and she was the perfect person to help me in that moment. Why I felt she was perfect for the moment was because she not only has the background of a psychotherapist, but she also has a spiritual component as well.

I believe that both Steve and Lesley were the people that facilitated the very beginning of gently dragging me out of that dark place and starting the process of moving forward. Together they were able to get me out of that bed and face one of the biggest fears we can ever face… and face it head on. It started with that first step - just getting out of bed. I remember it like it was yesterday, Lesley sitting at the bottom of my bed with me looking at her from behind the covers like it was all a dream… actually a nightmare… something that I surely would wake up from! Bless my husband for making that phone call.

In hindsight, we all know that staying secluded was not what happened. I obviously couldn't stay in my bed forever. I did end up sharing my diagnosis with my friends and family. That decision alone was very difficult. There was a very big part of me that wanted to just tell Steve and no one else. I really wanted to keep it a secret! My thought was that if I kept it as a secret, no one would have to go through and share the agony and pain of my diagnosis, the decisions to come, the scans, the process, the wondering "will Jill be okay?" I could spare them of their feelings on my behalf! *Yeah, that's a great idea! If I don't tell anyone else, I can just move along and do all of what needs to be done on my own. No one needs to know. I don't want anyone to be sad or worried about me.*

I'm sure there are many people who have been diagnosed with an illness or condition and have gone down the exact same road and then kept that kind of news to themselves. But I am actually happy, no…actually elated, that I DIDN'T make that choice. I truly believe that it's one of the main reasons I have done so well – sharing what I was going through with friends and family. The support I have received from family, friends, the community and even total strangers totally inspires and humbles me. In fact, thinking about it puts me in a state of awe and gratitude. It's been said that love and community goes a long way. The magic of what comes of that is quite literally hard to put into words.

Instead of staying under those covers, what happened took me on an incredible, fantastic and mind-blowing journey to the place where I am today. It affected my health on every level – physical, mental, emotional, spiritual. It has brought me to a place of peace and acceptance; a place of maintaining "being in the moment". It's the place from where I can hopefully help so many other people who are stuck, in whatever trial that life has thrown them. It may be some other form of illness or condition that a person has, or for that matter it may be that they just want to be more well! I've been told by dozens of people that I need to write a book as I went through my journey. What's funny is that every time I received that suggestion, I thought to myself *I couldn't write a book!* But here I am doing just that… writing a book about what I started calling "My Journey" and all the things I did which helped me to get to the place I am now. I believe it's an important part to why I am still residing here on planet Earth.

Throughout this book, I'm going to take you on my journey step-by-step in order to share some of the medical, holistic and spiritual approaches that I chose to take. Some of what you will read may seem very weird, strange or way out there! But as you read, know that this is **my** journey and **my** experience. If you keep an open mind, you will get more out of what you are about to read. Like I said, I honestly can't pinpoint EXACTLY what the reason is that I'm still alive. Nevertheless, I want to share the options that are out there that many people don't even know about. I want to share what I believe are the main reasons and the common thread that helped me to get to where I am today.

Should you decide to do the medical/conventional route of chemotherapy (chemo), radiation, and/or surgery, it's your decision. You may decide that you want to completely go the complementary/holistic route. You might even decide to do a combination of the two, which is what I did. Regardless of your decision, this book may help. My intention is to help you to find your way through whatever you're going through by sharing what I did. It is important for you to know that each person is different; each body is different. But the best part is that you **do** have choices. Some of it may sound familiar and, as I mentioned, some of it may sound just plain strange!

"The journey of a thousand miles begins with one step."

— Lao Tzu

The Beginning

I'm not sure where to say the entire journey started. Perhaps it started on the day I was born! If you believe that you were brought into this life to learn certain lessons, then that is indeed where it all started. But for the sake of honouring the different beliefs of each reader, my journey officially started on December 22, 2013 when I found a large lump just under the skin of my right breast. That's also a moment in time that I will never forget.

I was at my Dad's house spending a few days before Christmas, enjoying the pre-holiday season and, because I'm such a family person, enjoying the lead up to Christmas. When I first found the lump, I was surprised because it was so large. It was the size of a ping-pong ball. I thought to myself *oh it's obviously just a cyst... I've had so many cysts before.* In fact, I had a large cyst removed from one of my ovaries that was the size of a grapefruit when I was 18 weeks pregnant with my daughter, Lindsey! I also was told by the medical doctors that I had "lumpy" and what are called "fibrous and dense" breasts, so I thought *certainly it's just a cyst.* That being said, I wanted to be that "responsible person" and have it investigated. The day before Christmas, I walked into the local walk-in clinic because my own doctor's office was closed due to a flood!

The doctor there suggested I get a same-day ultrasound. Steve and I drove over to the ultrasound clinic and I had the procedure done. We then had to wait for the call with the results. It was like I could

1

hear every tick-tick-tick of the clock, as each minute felt like hours. In fact, that day was only one of many "waiting for results" periods that we would endure. We waited with hopeful minds during the day, but still feeling that gloomy feeling of what the outcome might be. The clock ticked but we continued enjoying the pre-holiday celebrations with our friends Karen and Craig. The phone rang only a few hours later as we were just wrapping up the frivolities of pre-Christmas cheer. It was the receptionist at the walk-in clinic. "Can you please come back to the clinic right away? We would like to see you back in here today if possible". I gulped and felt my breath stop for a moment. *Oh boy. That doesn't sound promising. It's the day before Christmas, I just had an ultrasound a couple hours ago, and now they want me to come back in before they close?*

Steve and I waited in the quiet room at the doctor's office of the walk-in clinic. We were the only ones there. We still felt hopeful and were joking around with each other and talking about our up-and-coming Christmas plans. We were trying to keep positive. In the middle of our jovial energy and conversation, the door quickly opened, the doctor breezed in and blurted out that it can't be good news if you're called back to the walk-in clinic the same day and just before Christmas! If you had taken a photo of Steve and my face after that ever-so-interesting delivery from the doctor, you would have thought he said we were both Santa Claus.

The way in which the conversation started made me feel surprised and taken aback to say the least. I felt my breath stop. He then told us that the lump was very "suspicious" and that they wanted to set me up to get a mammogram as soon as possible. We both walked out of that office feeling shocked and a sense of disbelief. It was so surreal. Since the mammogram appointment wasn't until January 2nd, we made a choice to keep quiet about this new situation. After all, the last thing we wanted was to alarm or worry anyone, especially since it was the holidays.

Time To Get the Biopsies Done – Pathology Never Lies

Mammogram day finally came. The results came back the same day and the clinic made a strong recommendation to visit the local hospital to get what's called a "mammogram biopsy" and an "ultrasound-guided biopsy". My experience was that these are two very invasive and incredibly uncomfortable procedures where they stick a tiny, long needle into the lump – 15 times to be exact (I actually counted). These would then be sent to pathology for further testing to find out whether the cells were cancerous (malignant) or not cancerous (benign). It was scheduled for January 21st. For almost three weeks we waited for that appointment, still hoping and praying that this was just some "misunderstanding" or that the medical doctors were being overly cautious.

Throughout the book, you may notice that I refer to the tumor in my breast as "the lump" or "bump". This is very much intentional. In my healing journey, I was determined not to bring any "negative energy" into my situation by calling it a "tumor" or a "lesion" or a "breast cancer lump". I made my mind up that these words would NOT be a part of my vocabulary, regardless of who I was talking to – doctors included. I would also never buy into the wording that so many use while going through this type of journey. For example, words like "battle", "fight", and "struggle" were not going to be part of my vocabulary since I wanted to keep the energy around my situation as positive as possible.

Steve and I drove to the hospital appointment on that cold January day to get the two biopsies done. Steve was asked to stay out in the waiting room during the procedure. As I lay on the cold, hard table the radiologist performed the procedure. It was nerve racking. I felt so vulnerable. Time kept ticking, ticking, ticking. It was a very long procedure. Through my discomfort, I watched her face to try to pick up a "sign". Nope. No sign at all. A funny thought went through my head: *She should play poker!* What a funny thought. I couldn't read her face while she worked away. It was so quiet that you could hear a pin drop. I laid there quietly, still hopeful that this was all just a big misunderstanding. Finally, she was done. She asked if I wanted my husband back in the room. We all know what the answer was to that!

She began speaking. She was very concerned about the largest of the three lesions on my breast. The large lump had "blood flow" and it appeared that it had a "tail". She strongly recommended that while we await the official results of these two procedures, I contact my doctor to schedule surgery. I remember lying there looking at the ceiling, freezing cold, with tears running down my cheeks. My husband was at my side. I could feel him gently holding my hand. I still thought *this can't be happening… this can't be true… I'm sure that this is all just a big mistake.* I remember feeling physically sick and scared. I couldn't even look at Steve. I was in shock of the possible outcome and all that was said to me.

For a full six days I waited and waited for those results. Each day I hoped and prayed that I would get the news that I was hoping for, but then came that fateful phone call. It still seems like yesterday.

After that time of being in bed and being "rescued" by Steve and Lesley, I was waiting for my doctor's appointment to see what would be the next step. I decided while I waited that I would use the resources I had at my fingertips – over twenty years worth of complementary health care practitioners that I have met through my own wellness business. *Surely there would be a way of going at this from a natural, holistic perspective!*

I immediately started making phone calls and started sharing the news with the many people I had in my circle. Just like you would imagine, I got many different opinions and many different suggestions. It was time to conduct some research to discover what resonated with me. Along with all of the suggestions, I made the decision to be very careful of my thoughts and how I spoke. Over the years, I have done a tremendous amount of reading and research on the power of the mind and our thoughts. I was sure that the things I did have control of were my thoughts and how I spoke. I was going to make sure that even in the darkest of times to come, I would be in control of those!

Divine Timing Or Just Plain Luck?
Yoga Instructor Training Program

During my experience of finding out about my new set of circumstances, I was in the middle of taking my Yoga Teacher Training Program. It had started in September only three months before I found the lump. Thinking now in hindsight, the timing couldn't have been any better.

For almost twenty years I had been helping many people through my own business. I was happy looking after clients with my complementary treatments like reflexology, Reiki and therapeutic touch. That being said, I felt like something was missing. Steve was the one who suggested that since I had been practicing yoga for almost thirteen years (and I was already in that type of business), that yoga would be a perfect fit to integrate into my wellness centre. He said that I would be an amazing yoga instructor. I was humbled and it didn't take me long to agree that this was a really great idea!

It was literally a blessing that the timing of events would have me in that course. I believe it helped me in so many ways. When I found out that I was "officially" diagnosed with cancer, I continued going to classes. I knew that yoga could only help. I really wanted to tell my teacher, Barb Leese . She has been my yoga instructor for many years and she was and is a great friend to this day.

At the start of the class after I found out my diagnosis, I sat on the little couch right outside the studio and told her the news. I tried to keep it inside, but the tears started to flow. It felt like a release actually. I didn't care who was there. In fact, the outside world seemed to stop for those ten minutes. Barb was kind, warm, and attentive as she always is. Her listening ear and gentle hug was just what I needed in that moment. As I delivered the message, I was still experiencing a very surreal type of feeling. *I can't believe I am actually telling my friend that I have cancer. When am I going to wake up from this bad dream, anyway?*

We sat there for those moments before the class, with Barb calmly, and with great conviction telling me that I would get through this. She said that I was a strong woman; I would find a way to get through it. Her encouraging words meant so much to me at what was such a fragile time. *She's right. I will get through this! I will find a way to get healthy.*

I didn't want to tell any of my classmates. Although I had already started bonding with a few of the people, I didn't feel comfortable announcing my news but Barb gently encouraged me to do so. She said that in times like this, getting support from old **and** new friends is very important. I trusted Barb. With her guidance and recommendation, I chose to walk into the classroom and nervously tell everyone my news. It is fascinating how different people take this kind of news. A few of the classmates immediately stepped forward to help and offer advice and kind words, another person said to me that he would have never, ever shared that kind of news with the class. The rest were silent. What's most interesting about the situation is that I believe none of the reactions were right or wrong, but rather everyone was reacting in the only way they knew how. One of the students actually came up to me after class and said "You got this, girl…you're not going anywhere". Jason is his name. We are still friends to this day. I still don't think he realizes the power of those few encouraging words he said to me that evening.

"Your soul always knows what to do to heal itself.
The challenge is to silence the mind."

— Author unknown

Extreme Self Care

One of the first suggestions I received was from a good friend and healer, Jennifer Lyall. In my session with her, she suggested a place in Florida called "The Hippocrates Health Institute". (www. hippocratesinst.org) During the first part of my journey, quite a few people mentioned this place. I didn't end up going there myself, but heard positive and incredible stories about the institute. I understand it is a fantastic place to go, especially if you are just learning about the complementary therapies available after having been diagnosed with cancer. Guidance is given on how to make changes in your life to help you get healthier. Apparently, they are excellent at teaching and helping patients get better. On their home page, there is big wording that says "Take Control", which really grabbed me!

Jennifer also suggested that I start using thermotherapy and recommended a "far infared mat." She emphasized that it was important that I invested the next part of my life towards extreme self care. *"Extreme self care"? What does that exactly mean?* Up to that point in my life, my world mostly revolved around everyone else, both personally and professionally. She suggested considering doing more things in my life that I love on a **daily** basis like yoga, hiking in nature, and "doing things for Jill". She also suggested that I receive different sessions and treatments from my holistic community. I made a choice to start using thermotherapy on a daily basis, continued my yoga and my walks with my dog on the Bruce Trail. I started making appointments with my team of comrades. I felt that it certainly couldn't hurt. That appointment with Jennifer was just the beginning of my healing adventure.

Jill Robinson

Naturopathic Doctor

Within a few days of my official diagnosis, I booked an appointment to see my naturopathic doctor, Dr. Melissa Howe, ND. She is an incredible naturopath and certainly shines in her field of expertise. At this point, the lump was already five centimeters in diameter. She gave me some suggestions such as eliminating animal products because of their burden on the digestion and kidneys. Animal products also contain hormones, concentrated toxins and often antibiotics. She also mentioned eliminating sugar consumption as there are many studies that demonstrate that refined sugar actually *feeds* cancer.

Additionally, she suggested I eliminate coffee and alcohol consumption, although neither of these were things I consumed a lot of anyway. She recommended that I start eating a "totally clean" diet, with organic food and no processed food. The intent is to encourage ways to help my body to be clean, unburdened and more "alkaline" rather than "acidic". There are also many studies that show cancer may feed on an acidic body. I actually was already doing most of what she suggested, but in hindsight, I still ate quite a bit of sugar and really wasn't eating as clean as I led myself to believe! There was definitely room for improvement. I really respect her.

That day, I decided to fine-tune my diet. I stopped eating refined sugar, drastically decreased eating dairy, gluten and meat. I drank no alcohol or coffee at all (although, as I mentioned, I didn't consume much alcohol or coffee). I increased organic foods when possible and focused on more alkaline foods. Interestingly enough, I lost 25 pounds in six months just from changing my diet.

Although she is a naturopath, Melissa is very supportive of medical intervention as well. She said that getting the x-rays, ultrasounds and scans that the doctors were suggesting was a good thing to do, as it would give me a good overview from a medical standpoint.

She did muscle testing (applied kinesiology) and discussed different foods, herbs, homeopathics and supplements that have helped other people through cancer. I used her infrared sauna as well. It was a wonderful experience. It actually felt like I was in Florida while I was in there! Like it was suggested at the beginning of my journey, she also mentioned thermotherapy.

Melissa suggested I make an appointment with another naturopath that specializes in women's breast health and cancer, Dr. Sat Dharam Kaur in Owen Sound, Ontario. It was worth going to another naturopath that had this specialty. I thought it was incredible that Melissa was referring me to get another opinion from someone whose focus was on helping women with breast cancer.

Melissa also gave me a huge "gift" of a different perspective of the diagnosis I had just recently found out. She told me that instead of looking at it as a "disease", I could look at it as a "dis-ease in my body", and that my body **does** have the ability to heal itself. *I had never thought of that before. It was such a different way of looking at the whole picture.*

During the appointment we discussed whether I was going to continue to work at my two part time jobs through my journey, regardless of what my choices were going to be. We discussed that many people choose to still go to their job(s) through their cancer journey, regardless of whether they do medical interventions, holistic options, or both. This decision was something that took some soul searching to decide. In hindsight, it was one of the most important decisions I had to make. Will I still work at my two jobs through all of what I was going to be going through? She suggested that I should consider taking time off "to take care of Jill". *What a concept. I was so great at looking after everyone else. I had helped to raise six kids in our blended family for many years, and both my jobs were helping people – I worked in my complementary wellness clinic helping clients and I worked at a large financial institution in the front line helping customers.* It was what Jill did best: looking after other people. *But what if that **is** what this new* *information is all about? What if this may be a time for **Jill to look after Jill**?* That concept was so bizarre to me. I had spent so many years giving and giving to everyone else and the thought of turning that towards myself was so…unfamiliar. It brought up feelings of guilt as well. *How could I manage doing this? What will it be like? Would I be judged? Is this even financially possible? What will "looking after Jill" on a full time basis actually look like…or feel like?*

After much soul searching, processing and discussions with Steve, I decided to do just that, take time off to get myself better. It was one of the best decisions I have ever made in my life!

Little did I know the road that would lie ahead of me…

First Surgeon Appointment – January 31, 2014

My general practitioner doctor referred me to a surgeon within four days. This was pretty incredible considering the waiting times for specialist appointments in this country and in this day and age. I remember sitting in the surgeon's office with my husband and my friend Tracy. She was doing very well after being diagnosed with fourth stage cancer in her large intestine, ovaries, liver and lungs. She decided to do the medical and alternative route and was even flying out to Switzerland for complementary treatments with the doctors out there. She went with me to the appointment to take notes and to be my sounding board since she had already been going through a similar path herself.

The surgeon began to explain that my current mammogram showed three areas of concern and I had what's called "ductal carcinoma". At this point, I was classified as having stage two cancer. She carried on to say that in about a week they would do a chest x-ray, a liver ultrasound, and a bone scan. In two to three weeks they would like to do an MRI of both breasts to check the left side as well. The treatment recommendation was chemotherapy (chemo) for three to six months before surgery to shrink the tumour, and then radiation after surgery. I was told radiation is done to ensure that any stray cancer cells left behind or "hiding" in your lymph nodes can get "zapped".

She recommended chemo before surgery because she felt the larger of the three tumours was too large and too high to be certain all would be removed during the surgery process. Plus, she was concerned that since the lump was so close to the surface of the skin, some skin would have to be removed, which would make it difficult to close the incision. After I heard all she had to say, I stared at her blankly. *Wait...I don't want chemo. I don't want radiation. Why are there no other options?* I told her politely that I wasn't ready to do chemo at that point and she was very respectful. I remember her smiling at me and almost confused at what I said, but yet very honouring of my decision.

She provided me with another referral to another surgeon in my area who could perhaps offer me a "non-chemotherapy" possibility. She suggested that this other surgeon had more expertise with this type of surgery and could do a technique that might possibly help me to avoid the chemo route. Before I left with the new recommendation, she manually checked me. I had no lymph node swelling, which according to my friend was very good news. The waiting game would be on again and despite feeling frustrated, I felt there might be a new ray of hope.

"The secret of change is to focus all of your energy not on fighting the old, but building the new."

— Socrates

More Appointments With My Comrades

While waiting for an appointment with my newly referred surgeon, I decided I would meet with my naturopathic doctor once again. We were going to go over a food plan and discuss what foods would support my immune system while at the same time listing which foods to avoid because they may actually feed the cancer. I found this very helpful. She also invited me to a seminar that was taking place later that week with a famous monk from Thailand who was known to help many people with many different types of conditions. I brought Steve along for the ride! He wanted to see what this was going to be all about as well.

This gentle, wise monk was incredible. After the seminar, he took time to talk to Steve and me, one-on-one and it was very informative. He talked about the importance of the power of our thoughts, which as I mentioned I was completely aware of and had been reading about for many years. He spoke of how important vitamin D was in cancer treatment. He went on to say that research supports the use of different kinds of Chinese mushrooms in the treatment of cancer. Despite his eastern philosophy and holistic opinions, he also strongly believes that medical advances are here to help us.

He said he knew people who made the same decision as I did, to do conventional/medical treatments, as well as complementary/holistic options. He said that they had done very well. For cancer patients, there can actually be a balance between medical and holistic options. *This makes sense. This really does feel right to me! Why **not** combine the two worlds?* He also said that my strong, healthy body and mind would help me get through this. Interestingly, he said that he felt that I am being taught so I can teach. At the time this sounded so strange. He mentioned also that there are many centres around the world that can support this type of decision and that their services are FREE. (see examples in the "Resources" Chapter at the end of the book)

A few days after that, I saw my friend Krista Campure. Krista is a registered massage therapist, Reiki practitioner, birth and bereavement doula and grief support worker. She is very passionate about wellness and is incredibly knowledgeable. She talked about vitamin D as well (I didn't tell her what the monk had said) and that there has been much research done on high doses of vitamin D helping patients with cancer and even helping with depression. We also talked about the fact that everybody takes news of a loved one having cancer in different ways and that we all react differently. After this fantastic visit, I had even more information in my tool pouch! It felt wonderful to be supported and get more information to help me make choices.

My good friend Sandi told me that right after she got my text outlining my diagnosis she "saw me" for a brief moment in a vision that had me in a running stance with the white baseball cap, a ponytail and pink on part of my coat. She said it was as if I were doing some form of crusade. She felt it was a possible "medical awareness" regarding my journey. If only I had known then what I know now. It's pretty amazing how true that has become.

While awaiting my second surgeon appointment, I also saw a complementary practitioner, Sarah Harper De Medeiros who is a registered massage therapist and Usui Reiki master. She also is a certified integrated energy therapist master, an axiatonal re-alignment master and does body memory recall. At the appointment, we spoke first and she said that she felt that this recent diagnosis was simply taking me on a journey to make me more powerful and strong in order to help others in a very big way. It's important to point out that this appointment was only **8 days** after I had been diagnosed!

When I laid down on her massage table, she said that it was most important for me to be as open as possible so as I could get the most out of the treatment. *I was ready to do the work! Whatever is going to help me get better!* Her treatment was incredible. I have never experienced anything like this before. During the treatment, I felt a very deep, intense grief and sadness that I've never experienced before. It revolved around the loss of my mother from cancer just a few years before. It lasted about an hour, but time got lost. Once we were finished, I felt exhausted, but definitely more clear, calm and relaxed. I really wasn't sure what had just happened, but I knew somehow that it was an important part of my healing.

> "You should sit in meditation for 20 minutes a day, unless you're too busy; then you should sit for an hour."
>
> — Old Zen Saying

Meditation - Time to Really Start Meditating...Like My Life Depended On It

As quoted from Yoga International (www.yogainternation.com):

> "The Real Meaning of Meditation – What is meditation? How does it work? Can meditation help you achieve genuine peace and happiness in today's hectic often chaotic world?
>
> Meditation is a word that has come to be used loosely and inaccurately in the modern world. That is why there is so much confusion about how to practice it. Some people use the word *meditate* when they mean thinking or contemplating; others use it to refer to daydreaming or fantasizing. However, meditation (dhyana) is not any of these.
>
> Meditation is a precise technique for resting the mind and attaining a state of consciousness that is totally different from the normal waking state. It is the means for fathoming all the levels of ourselves and finally experiencing the center of consciousness within. Meditation is not a part of any religion; it is a science, which means that the process of meditation follows a particular order, has definite principles, and produces results that can be verified.

In meditation, the mind is clear, relaxed, and inwardly focused. When you meditate, you are fully awake and alert, but your mind is not focused on the external world or on the events taking place around you. Meditation requires an inner state that is still and on-pointed so that the mind becomes silent. When the mind is silent and no longer distracts you, meditation deepens." (www.yogainternational.com)

I had been practicing meditation for quite a few years…well actually more "off" than "on"! I took a course on meditation in the early 2000's taught by Dr. Stéphane Treyvaud, a psychiatrist close to where I live. This particular course was called "Mindfulness-Based Stress Reduction Programs (MBSRP-X)" I learned a tremendous amount about meditation during that course. Some of the stigmas I had once believed were taken away. I learned that there are many forms of meditation and that it's about exploring the different kinds and finding what resonates with each person from their perspective. I also learned that there is medical and scientific evidence that supports the benefits of meditation.

It was interesting to learn that meditation can increase serotonin levels - a chemical in the body that is well known in the scientific, conventional and holistic communities as the "happy hormone". It can decrease stress, lower the heart rate and can quiet the mind. These are only a few of the benefits. The more you do it, the easier it gets, like working a muscle. Although I supported it, and regularly shared the idea with my clients, I really didn't do it very often nor did I enjoy it at all! Apparently, I wasn't practicing what I was preaching. Before my diagnosis, I would think *holy cow, this means I actually have to stop and slow down for some time! Isn't there something else I could be doing?* For some reason I had a belief that I always had to be busy. To this day, I'm not sure exactly where that came from. It was so solid a belief that I would book myself so busy that I would run myself down over time.

I even noticed it in my conversations with people. I couldn't imagine answering the question "how are you Jill?" without some reference to how busy I was. It really hit me one day when one of my teenage children said that they would love to walk in and see me reading a book or "just chilling". The thought of that mortified me! *I don't have time for that! There are so many other things to do!* But the truth of the matter is that my life **was** busy. I was helping to raise six children, all of who were **teenagers simultaneously** at one point. I also ran the house (including finances), was chief bottle washer, chef, nurse, counselor... well, you get the picture. I also had two part time jobs on top of that. The thing was, I rarely took time during the day "for Jill". I would hike with my dog in the mornings to help clear my mind. After that, it was time to run around and keep busy. When I think back to that time, I can't figure out why I thought I had to live my life like that.

Soon after my diagnosis, I realized that it would be a wise thing to "up the ante" on taking time for Jill, which included daily meditation. I began meditating every day for a minimum of thirty minutes. I knew that it could only help me. I would switch different meditations from day to day, depending on how I felt. I would either do my breathing meditation (see below), or guided meditations. There are literally thousands of audio (guided) meditations to be found. I had my favorites and still do to this day. under Meditation for examples). The trick is to be open to trying it.

Meditation can really only change your life in a positive way. In fact, over the years, I have suggested this breathing meditation to many clients and friends. Sometimes, I would make a suggestion to them – a challenge of sorts. The suggestion is usually for people that have a lot of stress in their life, for people that have a difficult situation they are dealing with, or people that want to improve their overall life and well being. My challenge/suggestion is this:

> For **seven days in a row**, do this simple meditation
> for only **ten minutes** a day:

Find a quiet, comfortable place to get ready for your ten minute meditation experience. Get yourself in a comfortable position where you are least likely to fall asleep (for example, lying down may not be the best choice since you may fall asleep – this would become napping, not meditating!).

Set a timer for the ten minutes so you aren't constantly looking at the clock. Once the clock has been set, just close your eyes and listen to your breath. Without judgment, just be aware of your breathing. Track it mindfully as the air goes into your lungs and then goes out of your lungs. As you are tracking and being aware of your breathing, attempt to slow it down. Try to keep it as even and slow and gentle as possible. Your mind will wander, simply because you are human. When you catch yourself thinking about something, and therefore not focusing on your breathing, just say to yourself, "That's interesting... I'm not being aware of my breathing anymore". Try not to be hard on yourself or get frustrated or give up. Instead, just gently go back to focusing on your breathing. What is most important is that regardless of whether your mind wanders one time in the ten minutes, or a thousand times, you are still mindfully going back to being aware of your breath.

Do this exercise for seven days, for ten minutes... like your life depended on it!

Then, once the seven days of the ten minute meditations per day are complete, you are to **not do any meditation** for the next full seven days. Not even one minute.

Finally, repeat the first week again: For a week, meditate once a day for only ten minutes.

This will therefore take a commitment of three weeks in total – ten minutes a day of meditation (on the two "on" weeks).

When I would next see the person after the three week challenge/ suggestion, we would discuss their findings. In the eleven years I have been suggesting this idea, of the people that did the exercise exactly as I suggested, **100% of them** said they noticed the difference and could see why people take time to meditate. That's a fact – 100%! What they noticed was that during the two weeks that they **did** meditate, overall they felt calmer, less stressed, less agitated, more peaceful and were able to handle the stresses in their life much better. On the week that they didn't do the exercise, meaning no meditation at all, what they noticed was that they actually missed the quiet time. They felt more reactive to stressful situations and overall didn't feel as peaceful.

Meditation and prayer is at the top of the list of what has helped me through my journey. In fact, I believe it is one of the main reasons I'm still alive today. I still make time to meditate at least thirty minutes a day, and even more if I am not feeling at peace with any given situation that comes my way.

"The secret of health for both mind and body is not to mourn
for the past, worry about the future, or anticipate troubles,
but to live in the present moment wisely and earnestly."

— Buddha

Who Else Did I See While Waiting For My Next Surgeon Appointment?

Psychotherapist

There is a very important psychological thing that happens when
someone has been diagnosed with cancer. In fact, it can be important
even for other diseases and conditions. Because I was on a mission to
get all the help I could to "get well", I started seeing my friend, Lesley
Hannell, the psychotherapist, on a regular basis. It was she who, at
the beginning of my journey, sat on the end of my bed! Although
at times it was difficult talking about what I was going through and
delving into the past, I truly believe it was an important part of my
journey. We explored why I may be angry, resentful, and sad. This
helped to peel the layers to get to my getting "more well" mentally.
She also gave me three meditation CD's that she made for her clients.
They are less than half an hour each and are "guided meditations".
These were a part of my regular routine to look after Jill. Regardless
of what you may believe, sometimes talking to a professional can
help you gain clarity and guide you through your situation. It did
just that for me. Keep in mind that sometimes it takes a few different
therapists to find the one that resonates with you.

Shiatsu Treatments Begin

I decided to start getting Shiatsu treatments from my good friend
Ann Crawford on a regular basis. I found that not only were her
treatments so incredibly calming and relaxing but she was also an
excellent sounding board to help me make my decisions. She has
such a gentle, kind, warm and supportive energy about her. My

thought was that I wanted to support my body with how much stress I was going through – both physically and mentally. This type of treatment could do nothing but help me on my journey to wellness. I saw her about once every four weeks and would greatly look forward to our times together. She gave me a CD of the Dali Lama chanting as well, which to this day I still use to meditate quite regularly.

Reiki Treatments As Well

I had been receiving occasional Reiki treatments from my friends Cheryl Mahon and Margaret R. for years. However, it felt like it was time to ramp it up! Like me, they have been practicing Reiki for many years. With my own research, I had heard that getting Reiki while undergoing chemo could be quite calming, relaxing and helpful. Cheryl is such a genuine and caring person. Margaret is such a dear soul and is so quiet, calm and caring as well. They both offered to give me Reiki treatments during my journey. After those sessions, I always walked away feeling so much more calm and relaxed, but most of all felt so cared for and loved.

Reflexology Treatments

Throughout my journey, I got regular reflexology treatments from my friends, Joanne Trumper and Sue Malley. I have been a certified reflexologist for over 20 years, so I know well the therapeutic value of a reflexology treatment. It felt right to get this done regularly to help my health. Right after I found out my diagnosis, I started getting treatments from these two incredible women on a more regular basis. Through my training and work as a reflexologist, I have had many other reflexology treatments of my own from many different practitioners. Although Joanne and Sue have very different techniques, they are each exceptional reflexologists. I still get regular treatments from both women for maintenance of my overall health. I like to explain getting "regular treatments" in comparison to owning a car. If you buy a car and look after it with the appropriate oil changes and tune ups then it is far more likely to run much better than if you buy a car and neglect it for years. Eventually, it will catch up with you. My analogy of the car can be paralleled with the care of the human body.

Naturopath that Specializes in Women's Breast Health and Cancer

My friend Simone Usselman-Tod and I did a five hour road trip to visit Sat Dharam Kaur, a naturopath who specializes in women's breast health and cancer. Simone's background made her a great person to take to my appointments. She worked in a cancer centre as an X-ray Technologist for over eight years. Her anatomy and physiology knowledge is incredible. She also is a massage therapist and has a holistic approach to life. That being said, her "gift" is to help people to clarify. She can help people to sort out the things that are confusing and help them look at **all** sides of the situation. To put the icing on the cake, she manages to stay neutral and non-judgmental. It was a two hour drive to the appointment so we decided to go up there together. Again, Simone was a great sounding board with her background, and really good company for the long drive.

My first impression of Sat Dharam was that of peace and beauty. She just emanated a beautiful energy of pure love and non-judgment. Simone and I liked her right away. We spent an hour and a half with her, going through my details, reports, scans, etc. She went over my history and results and gave me some more suggestions to help me along my journey of embracing the medical/conventional and holistic/complementary worlds of cancer treatment. She asked many questions.

She suggested getting genetic testing done to see if there was a genetic connection with the disease. Since my mother and grandmother both had breast cancer, it was important to find out if the gene for cancer would show up with this test. If it did show up positive, then there would be different precautions to be taken with my daughter and even my niece. We talked about hormones and how they affect women's bodies. She made suggestions of what herbs and supplements were **safe** to take during chemo. We talked about how stress and emotions both contribute to the wellness of a person. She strongly suggested I keep doing yoga as much as possible and meditating at least 11-31 minutes a day. We discussed my diet, which was very similar to what my other naturopath suggested, focusing on decreasing dairy, gluten, meat and refined sugar.

She suggested creating twenty "pictures" of who I wanted to become in my future. She suggested I write out twenty things on a piece of paper, like a "snapshot" of my future. Some examples for me were: having a perfectly healthy body, travelling, seeing my children get married and having children of their own. Basically it was like I was looking at photos in the future. This reminded me of something I learned many years ago called a "vision board", where you cut out pictures of different things you would like to attract into your life, and paste them on a board to be viewed daily. I chose to do this exercise on recipe cards – one card per snapshot.

She said to look at these "events/snapshots" for five minutes, two times a day. As I read each "snapshot", she suggested that I try to get an impression of what that feels like in the moment, as if it's already happened. She reminded me of the power of the mind and to imagine joy, purpose and optimal health for my body. Although this sounded a bit odd to me at the time, I chose to do as she suggested. It actually was quite fun and quite powerful! Some of the snapshots I wrote on those flash cards have already come to fruition…which is interesting and empowering.

Finally, she suggested a surgeon that she knew who specializes in mastectomies that involve the removal of tumours with or without removing the breast. She really respected and trusted this particular surgeon with carrying out mastectomies on cancer patients. It would turn out that he became my "surgeon number three". **As a patient, I didn't even realize I had the option to seek an opinion of a doctor in a different city.** Her referral was quite surprising to me. It's true, at least in our neck of the woods. With a referral, you can go to any doctor in our health care system to get another opinion, even if it's not in your same city. This was a very important piece to my journey. The sequence of events that led from this referral to see yet another surgeon, in a totally different city took me on a path that I still can't believe. I am so grateful for this!

It was a very informative appointment. I felt great and very positive as I walked out of her office with Simone. I had a ton of information to go over, and more choices to make. Regardless, I felt in control and positive moving forward. Simone and I discussed the appointment on the long ride home.

Intuitive/Healer

Between all the many appointments, I decided to book and see a dear friend of mine, Christine Riedel . I have known her for a number of years. She is very accurate and gifted in the work she does with the many clients she has seen over the years. She came to my house. Once we got caught up with each other's lives, we started the session. She told me that I am learning to focus on myself since for most of my life I have had an outward focus on everybody else and their needs. She said this process is about helping me to love myself.

She said my mom came through. This was an amazing experience. Even if you don't believe in this kind of thing, she was incredibly accurate on pieces of information she couldn't possibly have known about my mom or our relationship.

I never discussed any of that with her or anyone she knows for that matter. She told me I was being called to be a role model for others that are on this journey and that the journey is "far from being over". As you are reading this, keep in mind that this was only six months after my diagnosis. She said that rather than looking at it as a "fight", I could look at embracing the journey and that I have the opportunity to "love the cancer into non-existence". She saw me being a spokesperson for the community and the possibly the world. *Whoa.* She also said it's time for me to "play" more. *Sounds like fun!*

There was a lot more discussed in that appointment, but the bottom line was that I felt this to be very healing and helpful for me and my continuing journey. It was a choice that I feel helped more than I could have ever imagined.

> "Live life as if everything is rigged in your favor."
>
> — Rumi

Surgeon Number Two – February 26, 2014

I finally got in to see the second surgeon. I was excited about meeting her! It took almost two months after being diagnosed to get in to see this surgeon. To me, it was worth the wait. *Perhaps I wouldn't have to have chemo and radiation, but rather just take the lump out with surgery. Then I can just move on with my life and things can get back to normal!*

I walked into her office feeling a sense of hope that this path could mostly be complementary and holistic! My devoted husband went with me yet again, and along with him, my friend Simone. She would take notes and provide her perspective of the situation and write down what this "new" surgeon would say. She was going to help me so that I could make the best choice **for me.**

I sat in front of the new surgeon with hope. She was looking at my results and going over my history. After palpating my "lump", I could tell by her face that I wasn't going to hear what I wanted to hear. Sure enough, she stated that their "standard of care" options were to shrink the tumor with chemo first to ensure margins are as clear as possible prior to surgery. Next would be for me to receive radiation and then have surgery for a mastectomy.

She found that my lymph nodes were swollen under the armpit of the same side as where the lump was, and suggested an urgent biopsy of lymph nodes be carried out, to see if the cancer was spreading. I thought *can she tell by just feeling under my arm that the cancer was spreading?* As I sat there, feeling total numbness and dismay, I asked if there was another way, other than chemo. What about the naturopathic approach? She said that she had friends who were naturopaths and for the type of cancer I had, they would most likely suggest chemo as well.

I sat there feeling numb as she explained the effects of chemotherapy: hair loss, nausea, possibility of affecting the heart, and gut irritation. After palpating my lymph nodes, she made the analogy that the horses are already out of the gate. She went on to say that the problem is that there are no large clinical trials to prove that a naturopathic approach will help. She actually said to me that it is serious and if not controlled it will kill me. I could feel my mouth drop and my heart sink. My breath stopped short. *What? Ugh. That's not the news I was expecting!*

I left that office completely mad at the world again. I felt like I was outside of my body. I felt disconnected and furious. As I stormed down the hospital hallway, leaving Steve and Simone behind me, I thought that hiding under the covers again seemed to be an attractive option. *How can this be? Why is this happening? I don't want chemotherapy, but does that mean I am risking my life?*

The three of us talked about the appointment and after much soul searching and weighing my options, I decided I would start chemo but I would find ways to support my body while I was undergoing treatments. It still felt right to me to do both conventional/medical and complementary/holistic. *I feel great about this decision. It feels right. I will be fine. I am getting through this!*

Meeting the Oncologists – March 7, 2014

More than three months after finding that ominous lump, I sat in the cancer centre that was located in my area. As I mentioned, I felt this was the right thing to do. Steve and I waited patiently in the office. Both doctors were very pleasant. I particularly liked the younger one. She had a soft, caring nature about her that, despite my circumstances, I knew I would like. They told me that they recommend the type of intravenous chemo (meaning medication put into the veins) that you get once every two weeks for a total of three months. They would measure the lump before each treatment to ensure it was shrinking with the medication. I would lose my hair in about two weeks. At that point, I talked about my thoughts on doing complementary/holistic treatments while being on chemotherapy. I was told again that there are no clinical studies that support whether it would help me or, for that matter, interfere with the treatments. I had heard years ago that taking high doses of vitamin C and taking an herb called turmeric during chemo could be a contraindication to the effects of chemotherapy. I decided to politely be quiet, with the thought that I would discuss this with my naturopath in the very near future.

See the Naturopath Before I Start Chemo – March 14, 2014

A week later, I made another appointment with my original naturopath, Melissa Howe. Before I started chemo, I wanted to figure out how I could support my body. I shared with her that one of the surgeons I saw palpated my lymph glands under my arm and said they were swollen and therefore it could be spreading. She said that could be one option but that the other option was that they were swollen because my body could be just doing its job! She said that the lymph nodes can swell when the body is trying to get rid of toxins or unwanted invaders. I found this information very interesting. It was a totally different way to look at it.

We discussed all my options from a naturopathic standpoint but what was so incredible was that she said she would get the support of two other naturopathic doctors that specialize in the treatment of cancer. She explained that indeed there are natural herbs and supplements that could interfere with conventional cancer medication and treatments. She assured me that she would look into it and together we would support my body safely and carefully through what we both knew was most likely going to be a difficult time.

"Throw me to the wolves and I will return leading the pack."

— Author unknown

Time For the First Chemotherapy Treatment - March 18, 2014

The day came to start chemotherapy. Steve joined me on my first visit. We walked into the hospital, and I was ready to take on this adventure of getting medical treatment. I must admit that I was really nervous about starting treatment. I had been told what the side effects were going to be, but had no idea what to really expect. That day I was the rookie. Steve and I waited in the large waiting room area after I had my blood work done. There were a lot of patients sitting around waiting their turn. Some of them looked relatively "normal", but most looked very unwell. It was very difficult looking around at all the people. Upon observation, some looked hopeful and were talking and smiling and enjoying conversation with other people. There were many others that looked so distraught, so sad, so… hopeless. In that first appointment, I made a pact to myself that I would carry my head high and not only keep positive about my full recovery, but constantly have that sense of hope in my mind. I would not let anyone undermine this choice that I made.

Finally, after an interview with the pharmacist, getting my pre-chemo medication and a very long wait, my name was called. It was time. A friendly nurse with a bright blue gown took Steve and me into another area. There were people hooked up to intravenous and sitting in reclining chairs all over the place. Some were resting, some were reading, some were alone, others had someone with them. The friendly oncology (cancer) nurse prepared me efficiently and hooked me up to the intravenous equipment. I sat in the comfortable reclining chair under a couple of warm blankets nervously waiting for the treatment to begin.

Although the nurses were really friendly, there was definitely an "energy" about the place. To this day, I can't explain that energy… that tone. To try to describe it I would say that it was hopeful, yet fearful. It was positive, yet negative. There were two worlds being torn in this place, and if you let it get to you, if could be daunting and intimidating and frightening. That being said, I made a determined decision that I would not sit in the chair while they pumped the medication in my veins and think *this stuff is poison! What am I doing? I said I didn't want chemo and here I am!* No… absolutely not. Instead, I decided I would walk into that area with great positivity and listen to beautiful music with my headset on. I decided to meditate and read while getting treatment. But most importantly, as the oncology nurse was administering the bright red dye, I would think in my head *this is beautiful, good medicine going into my veins that is going to help me!* I imagined that the fluid going into my veins was like a stream of white, healing light and that it would do nothing but help me. *If the nurses could hear my thoughts, they would think I was nuts!* I didn't care. I was going to go through this with as much dignity and positivity that I could muster.

Over the next three months of treatment I stubbornly and positively kept meditating, doing yoga, and taking walks in the woods when I felt up to it. I continued doing my complementary treatments and taking my remedies and supplements that would actually support my body during chemotherapy but not interfere with the medication. I must admit that I certainly had my moments. There was intense tiredness, brain fog (feels like you have cotton in your head and your memory goes), nausea, and weakness beyond anything I've ever experienced. I remember after the first treatment, feeling like I had the worst migraine I have ever had in my life. My neck and shoulders were beyond stiff and I felt nauseous. I never once vomited though!

One of my "moments" is taken right out of my emotional journal after my second last chemo: June 12, 2014 - "I'm feeling tired, grumpy and down today. Sometimes I get annoyed and frustrated at all I'm going through, although feeling blessed to have fewer symptoms than most. I just will honour the moment and be okay with how I feel. Sometimes I think to myself 'I have cancer? How is that possible?' You'd think I'd be past that part by now. It's been six months, but I still find myself in a place of disbelief at times...I suppose that's normal...one moment at a time, Jill."

Mourning the Loss of My Hair – April 4, 2014

About two weeks into treatment my hair started falling out little by little. At first, there were noticeable strands on my clothing and pillow. The next time I washed my hair I ended up with a pile of my beautiful, long, blonde locks sitting on the counter of the bathroom. I remember thinking *It's just hair Jill. It will grow back. This is what is right for you. You can find a wig if you need to. It will be fine.* That being said, I cried that night. I was grieving the loss of my hair.

I looked so sickly with pieces of my hair here and there on my head. I clearly remember sitting in the chair at my hairdressers later that week and hearing the sound of the clippers humming. She was so sweet to book me in when there were no other clients at the salon. As I looked in the mirror and saw the straggly locks falling to the ground, I noticed two of the hairdressers quietly crying. *Wow. I feel so loved right now. It's okay, ladies! I'm going to be fine!* Of course, Steve was there by my side. My brother, Pete, sent me a photo text the next day, showing that he and his friend Mick had shaved their heads as well "to honour Jilly". It made me cry. It made me feel so much love and I felt so supported. That being said, I'm happy that all of my family and friends didn't decide to do that!

I decided to get a wig to wear during the time I had no hair. It took me a while to come to this decision. I didn't want to fall into a trap of caring what other people thought about the way I looked. More importantly, I wanted to stay in my authenticity that means so much to me. Many people who lose hair from chemotherapy treatments decide not to get a wig, but I'm so happy I did. I was referred to "The Wiggery" where the owner, Linda, made me feel so comfortable right away. Her warm, caring and kind personality radiated as soon as I met her. At first, I was very nervous and unsure of the whole procedure. My step daughter, Chelsea, went with me for support and to help me make a decision. We had a blast! We were giggling and laughing in no time at all. I tried on many wigs. With her many years of experience, and her obvious passion for her work, Linda found a wig very quickly that matched my own hair beyond anything I had imagined. When she placed the wig on my head, it looked so much like my "normal" hair. It was uncanny! It made me feel good. Because I'm the type of person that doesn't like to draw attention, I felt better in public with it on. I wore it to Chelsea's wedding. Again, I'm so happy I did! When I look at those pictures a year and a half later, I feel good about my decision. I didn't wear it all the time, but it was really nice to have the choice to do so when it felt right.

Overall, the chemo treatments went much more smoothly than anyone had expected. I was faring relatively well through the symptoms. The oncologist constantly told me that I was handling treatments much better than most. Instead of the symptoms lasting weeks, mine would last for a few days to a week. By the time the two week mark came I would walk into the next appointment almost feeling back to normal. On many occasions, my oncologist, and other doctors and surgeons for that matter, said I looked really good. One time she even said I looked radiant! During treatments, I obviously had my ups and downs, but overall my body was doing a great job at being strong.

The Three Months During Chemotherapy

During the chemo treatments I continued other complementary/holistic therapies. In fact, most of these treatments I did throughout my entire journey, not just during chemo. Additionally, I took the time to seek professionals and ask about what my options may be.

The therapies I chose to help me along my journey are defined in detail later in the book under "Definitions", but in general, I received, or did, the following therapies: meditation, visualization, affirmations, yoga, reflexology, Reiki, therapeutic touch, ThetaHealing™, ion cleanse, saw two naturopaths (one that specializes in cancer), shiatsu, infrared saunas and mats, therma therapy, John of God bed treatments, bowen, Quantum Psych-K, cranial sacral therapy, Ho'Oponopono, Lomi Lomi Bodywork, osteopathy, massage, energy sessions, healing sessions, psychotherapy, herbs, supplements, homeopathy, mindfulness, neuro-emotional technique (NET), chiropractic, traditional Chinese medicine, lymphatic drainage massage, hydrotherapy colonics, coffee enemas, and myofascial release.

I was so fortunate to have access to so many professionals in the complementary fields. As I mentioned, I was in that very industry for many years, so I had a professional circle of friends that gave me access to these disciplines. A few of the therapies and choices I made were free (for example meditation, visualizations, affirmations and yoga by myself). However, most of the modalities did cost money. The medical system here in Ontario, Canada pays for most of the conventional treatments for cancer through our taxes. This includes most drugs but not all of them. Most complementary/holistic treatments are not covered.

I was so grateful that I was also the recipient of four fundraisers set up to help me. Those fundraisers covered about two-thirds of what was spent for the choices I made. This was phenomenal and I'm so humbled and grateful for this "gift from friends, family and community". A few of the practitioners also offered me complementary treatments, which I am also eternally grateful for.

My personal view on this part of my journey is that, despite the stress of finding exactly how we were going to find the extra money, that my health is priceless. The bottom line: if you don't have your health, you can't live your life. We live in a finely tuned running machine called "our body". Furthermore we only have one body. There are no "reserve" bodies waiting on the sidelines...no "newer version" to be acquired if needed. We just have the one we were born with. My choice was to just find *some way* of acquiring the money. If I didn't invest in my health, I wasn't going to be able to live on planet Earth any more. It's a harsh reality, and I was willing to find ways to make it happen. My perception of this is that if you want it badly enough, you will find the way.

Fundraisers

As mentioned, during my journey four groups of people held fundraisers for me. The people closest in my life knew that the holistic options and treatments I chose to do were not covered by Ontario health care or insurance. As such, the decision to embrace holistic options was a huge commitment financially. I was going to find a way, nonetheless.

One fundraiser was done for my friend Nicky and me back in May of 2014 by the financial institute where we worked. It was so graciously organized by our managers and co-workers and was held in the style of a "Stag and Doe" that included donated door prizes and a silent auction. There was music (a DJ), food, dancing, a beautiful singer, and a cute little daughter of one of my friends, Sam, who did a few Irish dances for the cheering (and choked up) crowd of people attending. It astounded and humbled me how generous everyone was – friends, family members, co-workers, and even total strangers that didn't even know Nicky or me. As I type this, my eyes are welling up at how much it touched me. The love that surrounded us made me speechless (which would surprise many!) Sadly, Nicky passed away with breast cancer only two months following the event. I still miss her smiling face, her infectious laugh and how caring she was to everyone to this day.

The second fundraiser was held in November of 2014 by my good friend, Andrea Wilsdon, who owns a company called "Cindrea Brooke Jewellery" (www.cindreabrooke.com). She sells absolutely beautiful jewellery and organized an open house in which all the proceeds were donated on my behalf. She also donated several pieces of jewellery to the on-line fundraiser/auction. I wanted to show up that day, but it was a day in which I was feeling quite rough. Again, I felt humbled by how thoughtful people can be. I felt loved and supported by the generosity of so many people.

The third event was an on-line fundraiser/auction organized in November of 2014 by three of my friends, Simone, Janel and Heather. It was graciously set up in a way that there were products donated by many individuals, including a large community of holistic practitioners. Interested buyers could view the items and bid online. There was a date and time set for bidding to start and finish. The auction was closed at 9:00 pm sharp on the third day. The funds that were generated by this event were indeed astounding. I was literally shocked by how generous people were in donating and bidding on all the products and services offered. Many people were total strangers to me. They just wanted to help and to be a part of the cause. This fundraiser indeed was also humbling for me. Once again, the love that surrounded me put me in a state of awe.

The fourth fundraiser was done in December 2014. It was organized by the owner and the manager of the yoga studio where my friend Barb taught. It was a beautiful evening class led by Barb and filled with 40 fellow yogis and total strangers. Initially I wasn't going to go to the class, but Barb urged me to take part in it so I could feel the energy, love and support in the room. She further suggested that people would love to see me. I'm so happy I went. White twinkling lights softly lined the baseboards of the large yoga room as two musicians playing drums kept a mesmerizing beat that brought the entire room into unison. It was an incredible experience, beyond humbling with the gratitude I felt from the donations and support I received that night.

The love and support that I felt from those four fundraisers left me speechless. It's incredible what family, friends and even total strangers will do for someone. I felt so blessed. In the end, the money raised from these fundraisers covered about two-thirds of the costs that were incurred from the holistic modalities, treatments, remedies, etc. that I chose. The gratitude I feel for all those people involved will never be forgotten. It's what helped me so much to get through my journey on so many different levels.

Keeping a Journal

I kept two different journals – one in which I recorded every treatment and appointment I had regardless of whether it was conventional/ medical or holistic/complementary. The other was what I called my "emotional journal". In it I would often write down anything emotional I was experiencing during my journey. This was my friend Simone's idea. I'm so grateful she suggested for me to keep these journals! It's interesting as I look back at them and realize how much I really have been through. I was totally honest when writing in them. When looking back, some were barely legible as I vented like crazy! Other times, there was so much hope and things that made me laugh. Recognizing the importance of keeping journals not only helped me with writing this book, but helped me keep track of the timing of everything. More importantly, upon reflection, they helped me face my thoughts, feelings and emotions head on as things progressed, rather than burying them in a way that would no doubt have been unhealthy and counterproductive.

Neuro-Emotional Technique (NET)

When I was nearing the end of my chemo sessions my good friend Kimmy introduced me to Dr. John Millet. She said that he specialized in a modality called Neuro-Emotional Technique (NET). After her recommendation and hearing about the work he has done and the patients he has helped, I decided to book an appointment to see him. I liked John right away. He had a calm and caring demeanor about him. You could tell he was really listening to everything I was saying and truly was on a mission to help me. We discussed my diagnosis and all the treatments I had been undergoing. The appointment was fascinating. He did some applied kinesiology (AK) as well which helped to zero in on my getting the most out of the time we were together. I only saw John for two treatments, but I truly felt that he was an integral part of my healing and my "journey".

Surgeon Number Three – June 17, 2014

As I was monitored during chemotherapy, we could see the lump decreasing in size and that the two other lesions had actually disappeared! *Thank God* I thought. *Everything I am doing is working!* I remember that every time I went in to see my oncologist, which was once every two weeks, she would comment on how great I looked. I suppose compared with many patients, I did look different and healthier.

I met with the out of town surgeon during the last few treatments of chemo. This was the surgeon Sat Dharam Kaur, the naturopath that specializes in women's breast health, referred me to. It was a long drive to meet this doctor, but I really felt like it would be in my best interest to get that other opinion. He specialized in mastectomies. I felt that this was another important piece of the puzzle. There are surgeons who do everything from taking out your appendix, to cancer surgery, to sewing up a gunshot wound! Then there are surgeons that specialize in certain surgeries of the body. That settled my mind right from the start… knowing that for more than twenty years, this was all this surgeon did – mastectomies.

He also shared the option of reconstructive surgery. This was a surprise to me, since that had never been discussed before. The thought that I may be able to have this done was something I hadn't considered and wasn't sure how I felt about. It still gave me options and allowed me to make decisions of what was best **for me**. I took his advice and decided to meet with the doctor he worked with – the plastic surgeon. She gave me my options of best and worst-case scenarios and I decided I would book surgery with these two doctors in the hospital of the city farther away.

At this point, I decided to have the new breast reconstruction done right after the mastectomy. It just felt like the right thing to do at the time. I liked what the two doctors had to say and their approach to everything. Surgery to have the big lump removed along with reconstruction was scheduled. All was going smoothly. Or so I thought…

"I have not failed. I've just found 10,000 ways that won't work."

— Thomas A. Edison

Fast Growing Bump – July 9, 2014

Steve and I decided to go away for a week to sunny Florida with our time-share. It felt good to know that things were progressing well and surgery was going to happen. Taking a trip to Florida would be a great escape and it would be nice to unwind after all the chemo I had been through. I felt good about having surgery and, although other people may not, it was my choice. The lump was no longer shrinking in size so everyone agreed, from both the medical and holistic sides, that it was time to get it out. The conventional and complementary practitioners all agreed on this.

But, while we were away, something very strange started to happen. Remember, we were only gone for a week. The lump seemed to be growing…daily. Both Steve and I didn't say much about it, but in a bathing suit, it was hard to ignore. I remember sitting on the beach under an umbrella and thinking *Really? It's getting bigger again? And so fast! How is that possible? How can it be growing so quickly? This doesn't make any sense.* The fear in me was hard to ignore. In fact, I couldn't wait to get home. I was very scared.

This was taken from my emotional journal the day before we left to go home: July 9, 2014 - "I got out of the shower tonight and I could see the mass looks darker if I stand up straight. It's pushing against the skin. It looks like it's getting bigger daily. I am trying so hard not to worry, but I'm scared sh..less! I trust it's all in perfect order, but just wish the surgery was tomorrow. I want this "dis-ease" out of my body for good so I can move forward to being the new Jill and help so many people. I want to live! Please God; help me to get through this. Help me not to worry and fear so much. Help me trust that I am going to be well and look back on this as such a learning, healing time. I HATE being scared and insecure. It SUCKS! It's honestly the first time I wished time would hurry by (to surgery date). Will keep faith and pray and meditate and will contact the doctor as soon as we get home."

I contacted the doctors in the "farther away" hospital and they decided to do another MRI. Two days later, I remember sitting in my car in front of where I worked at the bank. My cell phone rang and the infamous "private caller" that would come in from the hospitals displayed on my phone. *It's the hospital. The MRI results have come back. What is going to be said to me? Why is the bump growing so quickly?*

The plastic surgeon's voice is what I heard. *Oh boy.* She told me that the surgery was going to be cancelled yet again. The team at the hospital all agreed that the lump was growing again and they strongly suggested that I see a radiation oncologist (a doctor who specializes in cancer radiation). I couldn't believe it. *I thought this was going to be done soon!* I remember sitting in my car and screaming and crying in disbelief. *How could this be happening? I have done the chemotherapy. The lump had shrunk! I just want this to be over.*

After eight months and all I had been through, I just wanted to move ahead in my life. I wanted to be back to what I called "normal". Soon after that phone call, I found out that after my MRI was completed, there was a big "meeting" about my case in the "out of town" hospital. At this gathering were medical doctors, the oncologist, a radiation oncologist, the surgeon and the plastic surgeon all in the same room. I must say that they were incredible at their due diligence! As much as I felt apprehensive about seeing yet another specialist,

I was worried about the size of the lump and that it was getting bigger…fast. I was in that appointment in less than a week, which is incredibly fast in the medical industry.

<u>Being Honest – A Dark Place</u>

It was after the surgery was cancelled for the second time that I was in one of the darkest places of my journey. Nights were always the worst. The fears and worries would come to the surface even stronger. I remember walking my dog to what's called "The Peak" which is on the Bruce Trail here in Ontario. It's a beautiful spot on the Niagara Escarpment where you can see the whole city. Some days, you could see for miles. One day, I remember standing there, contemplating life and all I had been through and looking over the edge. This is taken right from my "emotion journal": "…*woke up grumpy and down… realize today would have been surgery day. I walked PT to the peak…sat there for quite awhile…thought about how lucky I am to be able to walk there so briskly and not feel tired, for once. Also as I looked over the edge, I realized how I would never judge someone for taking their own life. I would never do it, but I can see how someone could get to that point. It was a bizarre feeling. I decided at that point to do something today to bring me joy.*"

Next Phase – Radiation …At the Hospital Far Away From Home – August 8, 2014

The meeting with the radiation oncologist went really well. I really liked this doctor. He had a friendly smile, was a great listener, and had this intensity about him that you felt like he would go way out of his way to help his patients. To be honest, when I think back to this time, the entire "away from home" hospital experience was very different from the first hospital that I was at. I'm not saying that one hospital is better than another, because I don't think that would be fair or even true. I believe they all truly care about their patients and only want to help. This hospital just had a different "feel" to it and with my being so sensitive to energy; the energy of this place was actually one of the first things that I noticed while being there. I also was told that this particular hospital was more progressive in some of the treatments it offered cancer patients.

After examining my history and examining the lump, the radiation oncologist said that he felt my best bet was to go at it very aggressively, because the lump was growing so quickly. The recommendation was to start radiation and do it two times a day, five days a week for 7-8 weeks and also to receive a type of chemotherapy once a week that will help "deliver" the radiation. He told me how the procedure would be done, what to expect and answered my questions about the procedure. One of the main side effects of this type of radiation is burning of the skin, pain and severe tiredness. I thought: *Is radiation part of what I need to do for myself? Does this feel right to me? And this would mean I would have to travel almost two hours twice a day on weekdays for 7-8 weeks!* That thought daunted me. *How was I going to manage this? I couldn't drive myself in case I felt weak or tired.*

He said he would put the orders in place for me to start as soon as possible, if I decided to go this route. Once he left the room, I told the nurse my concerns about living so far away and the commute I would be up against. *Would that be realistic? How would I manage that?* She immediately told me that if I chose to get these treatments at their hospital, there was a little "lodge" that was not far from their hospital, that is subsidized, making it reasonable for cancer patients to afford. Apparently, patients from out of town stay there all the time while receiving treatments. She said they have a shuttle bus that takes patients to and from the hospital from Monday to Friday and I could go home on weekends. *A little lodge? Sounds kind of quaint! Would I be able to handle living away from home during the week?*

I knew this type of treatment may be available in my own city but, as I mentioned throughout the book, my intuition and gut feeling told me that this is where I was meant to be. The whole concept of having this radiation was to get control over the lump that was in my breast. The lump was so large at this point you could see it through my clothing.

My journey was to continue with me living away from home. Although the people at the lodge I stayed at were quite nice, I felt that the inside was rather dated. When I walked through the front doors on the first day, I thought: *I'm not sure about this. What is the "vibe" I'm getting from this place? Could it be that it's because the people who are coming and going through this building obviously have cancer and therefore are getting some form of treatment? Or is it that when I look into the peoples' faces, I wonder if that person's going to live through their illness or not?*

I decided that despite my opinion of my accommodations, I would bring my own world to my little room. I brought inspirational posters, pictures of the beach and photos of my family. My brother's girlfriend, Cherry, bought me a beautiful bright, happy-looking and colourful comforter that brightened the room as soon as it was placed on the bed! I felt this was so thoughtful.

I had a roommate, Linda, for most of my stay at the "lodge". She was an amazing woman; very positive and down-to-earth. Despite the fact that I really thought I wanted to be on my own, I really enjoyed her company throughout the process. She had an amazing sense of humour and called me "Roomie" all the time. Sadly, she passed away when I was at the tail end of writing my book. I only knew her for a few weeks, but we bonded right away. She was an important part of my journey.

The shuttle bus would take about 15 minutes to half hour to get to the hospital, depending on the traffic. On my first day, I was very nervous about what was going to happen to me. The actual radiation treatment process itself took only minutes. The people that were looking after me, such as the nurses and the radiologists, were incredible, attentive and caring. They were fun and uplifting and always joking and making me feel welcome and cared for. It made what could have been a very down and depressing experience incredibly happy and easier to handle. In the first couple of weeks, I thought *hey this is a breeze! I don't feel anything while the treatments are going on and yah, the skin feels a little bit irritated afterwards but no big deal!*

My story changed in week three. The skin started to get red and burned and felt itchy and irritated. It kept getting worse and worse. My tiredness got worse by the day. Near the end of all the treatments, the pain was worse than any other pain I have experienced. Despite being managed with pain medication, it was beyond anything I had ever experienced. It made childbirth look like a picnic in the park. It even made chemo look less intense. Regardless, every day I would wake up, travel to and from the hospital twice a day in the bumpy shuttle bus, lay down on the cold, steel table and allow the process to continue.

Near the last few treatments, I remember a moment of time when I stood in front of the bathroom mirror, completely naked from the waist up in my little room. I was in so much pain from the treatments that I was on a low dose of morphine. Nothing else would take the pain away. I had tried so many types of pain killers – some giving me horrible hallucinations. The area where the treatment was directed was bright red and constantly throbbing and it was swollen up like a big, frightening balloon. I was applying the salt solution and cream that they had suggested to help with the burns. *I can't do this anymore…this is just too much. This hurts too much and it's too painful. Remind me why am I doing this? Why am I here?*

This was taken from my emotional journal during the last few treatments: September 24, 2014 – "I struggle with the balance between the symptoms, pain, extreme lack of energy, and what my body is experiencing from this treatment. At what point do I say 'enough is enough'? They (radiation technicians) mentioned even longer treatment time because my skin is still intact and the lump is showing via ultrasound that the treatments may be working. I'm in pain constantly, from burns to internal pain to incredible fatigue. I admit that there is a huge part of me that is DONE. I just want to have surgery and start the process of healing from that. It's been nine months and I feel like it's been a marathon. I know my body is super strong, but I waiver between the benefits of this treatment 'saving my life' and the energetic/spiritual component to the big picture. If I totally relax into the present moment and trust the process, then I shouldn't care if I have more weeks of radiation. And I have that thought somewhere up there in my mind that I don't want to cut short anything if it's going to compromise what I want to do with staying in this body to enjoy my life with myself, Steve, the kids and to help so many people. This is a conundrum that is worthy of discussion and also to go within Jill to ask."

Another entry taken only five days later: September 29, 2014 – "I'm feeling like crap today. I met with the radiation oncologist and they feel I should do another four more rads. I'm in so much pain and Tylenol 3 barely touches it. So tired. In bed all day Saturday and today. I'm swollen up like a big, red balloon. I'm questioning everything. Things I shouldn't be thinking about. Having faith and trust is at its peak now. Totally weird feeling. I miss Nicky and Tracy (these are my two close friends that had died recently of cancer). I know it's their journey, but it's daunting. So tired of all this. Done. Just want all of this to be finished, move on with life in a happier, healthier 'new Jill' place. No appetite today. I'm physically and emotionally finding this challenging. Need to be honest, so here I am. It's tough but I want to be authentic." (I could barely read my own writing at this last quote)

It was an incredibly difficult time. I thought I'd never get through it. I remember feeling angry, scared, concerned and upset. I was being true to my feelings. What kept me going was that famous word – hope. It also was the positivity of having my family and friends that wanted what was best for me, cheering me along. It also didn't hurt that, when feeling up to it, I was reading books that were inspirational.

One particular book I was reading was by an author in my area. The book is called "Ask and You Shall Receive: Embracing Hope" by Karen Zizzo. I have never met Karen, but her book was amazing. This quote from her book was entered into my "emotional journal": "The clinical diagnosis, and the way in which it was presented to us, could have taken away all shreds of our hope (on the diagnosis of neuroblastoma in their seven-year-old son). We realized that no one had the right to take that away. There is always hope. There's always a chance that things are not as they appear. There are mistakes, there are miracles, and there is the power of prayer. No one person can accurately determine the outcome. You truly need to hold onto your faith, and your hope, and you must trust in the power of your own belief in something beyond this world." (page 12 from "Ask and You Shall Receive: Embracing Hope" by Karen Zizzo)

Finally, when the doctors changed my pain medication and I was almost done treatments, I wrote this in my emotional journal: October 2, 2014 – "Feeling more human today. It's amazing how pain can make you so loopy and distraught. I do feel calmer and less edgy today, but pain is still there, but manageable. It's amazing to me how we as humans can so quickly go to the negative in situations, despite being "evolved" or "spiritual". That fascinates and intrigues me. Part of this is to remind me that I AM human and despite how well I'm doing overall, I'm giving myself PERMISSION to be angry, scared, concerned and upset and that is all perfect in its own right! It's part of being human, authentic and real…not just with others, but mostly within myself. To be honest about how I really feel, rather than sugarcoating it that it's all fine. It's the Ying and Yang part of being in this human shell. I'm being reminded to love myself no matter what and that I am perfect just the way I am."

Family and Friends

There were many, many appointments that included the "out of town" hospitals. Steve was always at the appointments where I needed to make decisions or when there were going to be results given to me. He was incredibly supportive throughout my journey and was beyond attentive in every way. My dad was the person that did a lot of the driving. He was there for me like no other father could be. He constantly offered to help me and drove me for many miles to appointments in his little Honda while encouraging and supporting me. He looked after me at the house for many hours. I thought at the time: *This is all backwards! My Dad is in his 80's… aren't I supposed to be looking after **him**?* I realized that despite age, we are there for those we love in times of need. He was so helpful in my time of need. I appreciated his help and support more than I could possibly write in words.

Each of my six children supported me in their own ways. At the beginning of my journey, their ages ranged from 19-26. Three of them lived at home at the time. The other three had already moved out. They all handled my diagnosis and what I was going through differently and in their own unique ways. There was help with our dog, warm texts, loving visits, words of encouragement, dinners made, gentle hugs and so much more. I will never know exactly what it must have felt like to be a child of a parent going through what I was going through. I'm sure there was more going on behind the scenes than I realized. Each of them showed a level of care, love and concern that made me very proud.

I also had tremendous support from my other family members and friends. Their help would be anything from helping by making food for me, driving me to appointments, talking on the phone or uplifting visits, texts of encouragement, and of course the fundraisers I mentioned.

In the weeks that I lived away from home to get the radiation, I spent time with my only sibling, Pete. I remember fondly that we made a pact that every Wednesday we would get together because he worked so close to where I was getting treated. He would pick me up after my second treatment of the day and we would drive through crazy traffic and stay at his house for the night. Early the next morning, he would drive me back in time for my first treatment. I loved this arrangement. It meant I could spend time with my brother, his girlfriend, and my niece and nephew. This helped in making the five full days away from home feel less long.

I warmly remember the beautiful talks that we had in his car, sitting in the bumper-to-bumper traffic, and the sense of family and love that I got from it. It definitely increased the closeness that I felt with my brother because of that one-on-one time together. Even though some people would say that what I was going through was a "horrible" or "negative" experience, there were waves within it in which I got more appreciation of life and more appreciation of those who loved me. If I didn't spend those weeks in the city away from my house, my brother and I would never have spent those hours in the car in traffic together. And I don't believe we would be as close as we are today.

I often thought how different the path would have been had I made the choice to keep my situation to myself. What a beautiful gift to be given love and support at so many different levels. I have thanked all who supported me, family, friends, practitioners, etc., so many times. I still have difficulty describing the intense gratitude I feel for each and every one of these people.

"You, yourself, as much as anybody in the entire
universe, deserve your love and affection."

— Buddha

Wellspring Cancer Support Centre

During the two months of radiation appointments, when I felt up
to it I would enjoy short walks while awaiting my treatment times.
One beautiful sunny fall day, I stumbled upon a cute little building.
On the wall outside the front door was a sign that said "Wellspring".
I wonder what that place is all about? I had to wait another hour for
my treatment so I decided to go inside and find out.

I walked through the front door and I immediately felt welcomed. It
was bright, well decorated and had a very warm feeling to it. There
were smiling faces everywhere I looked! A lovely lady who was sitting
behind a beautiful wood desk greeted me with a warm smile and
asked how she could help me. I embarrassingly said that I wasn't
really sure. I told her that I was receiving radiation treatments and
just decided to see what this place was all about. With a big beaming
smile, she gently went on to explain: "Well, welcome Jill! Wellspring
is a beautiful, warm and welcoming facility that offers a variety of
supportive care programs, at no cost, for cancer patients and their
families. There are other Wellspring centres in other cities as well.
We provide emotional, psychological, restorative and educational
support programs and services." *Wow. This place sounds so amazing!*

She went on to share that they have everything from art and music
therapy, cancer support groups, counseling, meditation to cooking
classes. They also offer therapeutic touch, Reiki, yoga and QiGong.
Oh and there were professional speakers that came in regularly to
help people going through any kind of cancer. *This place is like the
best kept secret! There are so many people that could benefit from this
incredible place!*

I suppose you've already figured out that I became Wellspring's newest fan and advocate. I started telling anyone who would listen about this place that offered cancer patients (and their families) help along their journey and, best of all, everything was FREE. I carried pamphlets around with me all the time.

During my visits to Wellspring, I would sometimes just sit in one of the big, bright, big-windowed rooms and just rest. There were also times that I would read, or close my eyes, meditate, eat my lunch or take my remedies. I also attended a few of their classes which were all wonderful. I took a vegetarian cooking class, a gentle yoga class, attended meditation circles, and one evening I attended a free seminar on reconstructive surgery which was very informative!

This was taken from my emotional journal while resting in a room at Wellspring: September 2, 2014 - "I'm really becoming more aware of how much I enjoy quiet, stillness and down time. It's so good for my soul and spirit. I wonder often why I thought I had to keep so busy and moving and doing…it so perplexes me at this point! I never thought I'd say that this 'process' has been a blessing to change my life in ways that I never would have imagined".

One day, when I was about half way through my treatments, I was sitting meditating in what became my favorite room at Wellspring. I was calmly sitting on the comfortable couch and I had an epiphany. At that point, I had already been aware of the power of love - the concept that "love can conquer all" and how important positive thoughts and energy could be. With that in mind, I made a decision: Instead of being afraid of the large lump in my chest and what it represented, I would actually **love it**. Now some of you may be thinking, what kinds of drugs was Jill really on at that time? I would chuckle at that and say, "not the kind you would think!" It simply was a choice I made. It's a choice that felt right to me, and with all the research and reading I had done on the subject, it just made sense. I didn't share that with many people, probably because of how it might be received, but mostly because I didn't want the opinions from others to influence what felt so sacred and important to my journey.

Epiphany aside, I would highly recommend looking for a Wellspring in your area. If there is not a Wellspring, check to see if there are other centers that offer similar free services and support groups to cancer patients and their families. Without a doubt, it made my experience at the hospital so much better. It became one of the most powerful spiritual components of my journey.

(For more information on a Wellspring Cancer Support Centre in your area, contact www.wellspring.ca.)

Part of a Study While Going Through Radiation

At the beginning of my radiation process, I was asked to be a volunteer as a part of an ongoing study and research project at the hospital. They would do a weekly ultrasound of the lump to see the "progression" of the radiation treatments by utilizing a new ultrasound program. With this new kind of ultrasound we were able to see if the tumour cells appeared to be dying and to take accurate measurements of the lump. I suppose in hindsight it wouldn't have been a good experience if the weekly ultrasounds were not indicating that the radiation treatments were working in a positive direction. As it turned out each week it looked better and better which gave me a sense of hope. I was told over and over again, that this was just a research project and only a study by the kind technician. But nevertheless, it gave me a sense of hope and somehow I felt more involved in my care.

I was even asked by the hospital if I would be one of twelve people to be interviewed to give feedback on what I felt about this particular type of tracking. I was very passionate about doing this video interview because I wanted people to know that being followed like this can be very important in the process. What is one of the most daunting parts of going through this type of experience is the not knowing where you stand and (obviously) not being able to see inside your body. It can feel helpless when you don't know if the treatments you are receiving are working or not. Of course you always have the hope that they are working to get rid of those unwanted cells, but to have somebody look at it visually, that knows what they're doing, who is experienced with this type of thing, meant a lot to me at that time.

I am very grateful for that experience and time while getting treatments and mostly I appreciated the positivity and warm care I received by the ultrasound technician who was responsible for the study. He was a very special person and I would look forward to our chats and our time together. He truly cared about my well-being and was fantastic at explaining things to me. He went over the top to help me and make my experience as stress-free as possible. He constantly was open to answer my questions and concerns. He made a huge difference while I was receiving the radiation treatments. I will never forget all he did for me while I was there.

New Oncologist at the Hospital Out Of Town – August 13, 2014

Because I was getting care in a new hospital, which included radiation treatments and possible surgery, it was suggested I see their own oncologist so that I could be followed within their own team of doctors. This made sense to me. Again, Steve and I drove the almost two hours to yet another appointment. After speaking with the oncologist, she shared that, in her opinion, I was doing the right thing. She told us that she would never recommend reconstructive surgery because of the type of cancer I had. *That's interesting. So different than what the other doctors had said.*

As I had done many times before, I discussed with honesty the fact that I wanted to be supported in my journey with holistic and complementary approaches. As I had heard so many times before from the medical industry, their professional perspective could not verbally agree with what I wanted to do. Again, from their point of view, there were no statistics to prove whether or not they would contraindicate each other. In other words, they were concerned that the "complementary or holistic" choices would impede the work the medicine (chemo and radiation) was doing. I do remember her saying that the type of cancer I had is a very "tricky" cancer. *What does that really mean – "tricky"?* It wouldn't be the first time I heard that my case was not common.

Knocked Down Again - October 8, 2014

Eight weeks and 58 treatments of radiation later, I moved out of the "lodge" and back home. It had now been ten months since I was diagnosed. It was glorious to be back in my own bed, to not have the thought that on Monday I would be heading back out of town for my treatments. Although the lump had not shrunk at all during that time, and was still the size of a tennis ball, the ultrasounds gave the impression that what was left were only dead cells (necrosis) and fluid. *That is fantastic news!* The only way to find out for sure was to have it removed and sent to pathology for testing.

After the agony and pain I experienced in the last weeks of radiation treatments, it was time to see the "out of town" oncologist. She was going to give me the recent scan results after the radiation was complete, to assess how things were doing. Because I was driving from another city, they had set a same day appointment with their surgeon. Surgery was on the table again. It was finally time to take that large lump out of my body and also have it tested.

Steve and I waited in the small examination room for the oncologist. Waiting for appointments had become a very familiar part of the process I was going through. We waited for a very long time before she finally walked in. But, instead of just her, a number of additional people followed her into the room. By the time they all flowed in, there were six people including Steve and me in that little hospital examination room. I recognized the oncologist, the nurse, and I knew the other person was the surgeon. The person I didn't know turned out to be a resident of the surgeon. I felt my breath stop for a moment and my heart sank into my stomach. *Wait a minute? This appointment is just with the oncologist. Why is the surgeon in here too? That appointment is for later on today. What's going on?* My heart began to race.

They all looked very stern and concerned. *Why is this not feeling right?* The oncologist pulled up a chair and sat right in front of me, only about two feet away from me. The others quietly stood against the wall behind her. One was holding a chart. But what really struck me was that most of them had their arms crossed. *Oh man. This doesn't feel right.* She told me that unfortunately the new scans show two lesions on my right lung. By the radiologist report, it looked like the cancer had spread to my lungs. She said she was very sorry to have to tell me this new information and that they all agreed that it would not be in my best interest to have surgery.

They wanted to change focus and would be sending me back to my "home town" oncologist to discuss my options. She also told me that I was now classified as having stage four cancer because the scans showed it had metastasized (meaning it had spread to another organ). I felt sick. *How is this possible? Is that report correct?* My stomach was in knots. I couldn't even look at Steve. They left the room very somberly after all saying "sorry" to me. Steve and I barely looked at each other. We quietly exited the room, left the hospital, and hardly said a word in the car. Since we were so close to my brother's house, I insisted we still go there since we had planned on stopping by on our way home. Perhaps it was my stubbornness and wanting things to "go forward as usual", but I was determined to carry out our night as planned.

When I walked into my brother Pete's house and he walked towards me, I totally lost it. I started crying my heart out. I felt defeated. I blurted out the latest news through my wavering, unrecognizable voice and tears. He said nothing as he held me. We cried together, as he held me tighter than I had ever felt him hold me before. As I looked over his shoulder, I noticed that Steve and Pete's girlfriend Cherry were doing the same thing – crying and holding each other. To say it was a very sad scene is an extreme understatement.

After what felt like a very long time of standing there in the hallway at the front door in a very surreal moment of time, I suddenly felt a rush of a thought. *Wait a minute! This **is** really happening, but it doesn't mean it's a death wish! I'm still here! I still have options! I am not giving up!* I gently pulled away from my brother and while wiping my tears away, announced that "we weren't going to talk about this anymore tonight. Instead, we are going to carry on and enjoy the evening the best we could."

I remember watching Steve that night. He looked like he had aged ten years in a matter of hours. He was very quiet, his shoulders were hunched over, his eyes were red and there were lines of worry embedded in his face. He actually looked defeated. I couldn't even **imagine** what he was feeling. As I looked across the room, I felt like I wasn't in my body. I felt like I was physically in the room...but not really there. Pete and Cherry were quietly getting dinner ready. My niece and nephew were doing their thing like normal kids do, although they were much quieter than normal. Steve looked like someone had died. It was a moment that, although I felt intense sadness to see him this way, it actually made me stronger. It made me feel more stubborn to keep believing I was going to pull through. I thought *I have read and heard that there are many people that have been in my exact similar situation, and they are still alive! I am going to figure this out. I have way too much living to do. We are just starting our lives together again after raising six children! I can do this!* I felt a rush of positive energy come over me in a wave. I was going to continue to figure out what choices I had and most importantly, not let fear and the unknown dictate how I felt.

"Vitality shows in not only the ability to persist but the ability to start over."

— F. Scott Fitzgerald

Moving Forward

I went back to my home-town oncologist to let her know what had been going on. She suggested that I go on chemotherapy yet again, because of the concern that it may now be spreading. Instead of doing the intravenous route, she gave me the option to take oral (by mouth) medication. She explained that the side effects weren't the same as the other type of chemo. I wouldn't lose my hair, but I could get numbing and/or pain in my extremities (neuropathy) and/or get blisters on my feet. Despite the possible side effects and with my holistic mentality, I decided to go home with the prescription. I would "get still" and "go within" to see how I felt about this new option. Of course, I also discussed it with Steve and a select few of my comrades. I decided to start taking the oral chemo. *I don't want to take any chances.* I still wanted to see if I had other holistic options as well.

The side effects of the oral chemo were quite painful and concerning. I did have the neuropathy (numbing) of my fingers and toes. My feet were so painful; I had difficulty walking at times. The doctor altered the dosage. This helped. And although I decided to embrace this new type of chemo, I also decided it wouldn't hurt to seek the advice of a Traditional Chinese Medical Doctor (TCM). I had heard many other stories about how this type of treatment had helped cancer patients.

Instead of going to a random doctor, I remembered a friend telling me that she knew someone who had breast cancer and it disappeared after being treated by this particular doctor and his Chinese herbs. This person didn't have cancer anymore. The scans were clear and the medical doctors all said it was a miracle. It was worth a chance. His office was only fifteen minutes from our house. Again, I wanted to see what my options were. I just wanted to hear what he had to say. It was a choice.

I made the appointment with the Traditional Chinese Medical Doctor that my friend told me about. He was a very quiet, gentle man. I remember he had a very warm smile and an infectious laugh. At times, it was difficult to understand some of what he was saying with his heavily accented English, but I deciphered most of what he said. He said the key to getting better and getting rid of cancer is by building up the immune system "so the body can fight this invader". He suggested ten different herbs to take daily to help support and boost my immune system. He told me to avoid shellfish, peanut butter, fried food and Canadian hamburgers (which I found quite amusing). He also said to me with a beaming smile "keep thinking happy, positive thoughts! Believe you **will** be well…don't stop doing that!" *That was very interesting. I didn't even tell him I was already doing that!* He also said that taking the herbs would not interfere at all with the chemotherapy. He had treated many patients over the years that did both medical and holistic therapies. He actually supported combining the two worlds of treatments. That felt wonderful.

Medical Intuitive

I shared my recent dismal news and scan results with my good friend and Shiatsu therapist, Ann. She told me that her friend, Carol Pearson Shaw was coming to visit her clinic. Carol is what some people refer to as a "medical intuitive" or "healer". I had seen her a few years before. She has a very good reputation, and her work was very accurate with her many clients. As I mentioned before, I was willing to try whatever it took to help me get through what I was going through. I had so many choices and I thought to myself: *What do I have to lose? I can book the appointment, hear what she has to say, then I can see if it resonates with me.* I soon had another thought: *I hear that she will not hold back in her delivery when she sees clients (meaning that if she "sees" a "concerning" or "dangerous" situation in your body, she will tell her client that as well).*

I had heard that she had "found" things in many of her clients' bodies and when they went to their doctor, it potentially saved their lives. I am aware that this may sound very strange to many people, but I ask that you keep an open mind and make your own choice to believe it or not. Either way, I wanted to hear what she had to say. I set the appointment, which was coming up soon.

She is such a beautiful person; so gentle and loving. I met Carol at Ann's clinic. After a warm hug she sat down across from me. It's important to note that I didn't tell her ANYTHING about the details of my situation. All she knew was that I had been diagnosed with breast cancer…that's it. She looked at me quietly. Actually at times it looked like she was looking through me! She said that she didn't see anything concerning and that the two little "suspicious lesions" on my lungs looked rather like burns in response to the radiation treatment itself! *What? Really?* The frustrating part is that, to this day, I will never have proof of whether that's true or not. But I find it really interesting that I didn't even tell her that when I had radiation it wasn't just on the lump itself being targeted by the radiation.

I didn't tell anyone other than Steve, for that matter, that when I had radiation it was over a much larger area than just where the lump was. She also said not to be concerned about the large lump that was at the surface of the skin on my right breast. She went on to say that it was so beautifully encapsulated, with no leaks in it and the cells inside were dead. It appeared like it was like a rubber ball. Does that sound weird? Maybe so… but what's so uncanny is that she described that "lump" almost **exactly** the same way as the doctors had recently described it from the different scans I had done!

She also mentioned that the most important part of my journey is to attempt not to go into fear, but rather to feel joy and peace. To know that innately **our body knows how to heal itself** and that my upbeat personality will certainly help. She suggested I do affirmations. One of the affirmations that she suggested for me to say was:

> I am a divine being. My body is a divine temple. My body understands how to heal. I have absolute trust and faith in my own body and my own abilities.

Another affirmation was:

> There is no invitation and no place for disease in my body. My body is a divine temple. It can no longer support any disease or any abnormal cells of any kind.

She also told me this could be observed as an exciting experience; to have no attachment to it, but rather have a sense of "letting go" and moving through this as simply a life experience. Some people that would hear this statement may think this sounded crazy or even take it negatively. But it actually resonated with me. It made sense. Again, I was open to whatever it took to help me get better.

She continued that there is a lot of freedom in "letting go". My task is to not take on others fear and energies. This is why I was so very careful at how I allowed people to speak to me and how I spoke for that matter.

She also mentioned that I'm role modeling a particular way of being and suggested to speak and act as if I'm **free of disease**. I really liked this concept. It was a concept I was already familiar with. It had to do with energy and behaving as if my "perfect health" had already come to fruition. She said another vital part of the healing is to **receive with love and gratitude** and just **say thank you**. This was a strong turning point for me in my journey. It solidified my belief in the importance of thoughts, taking responsibility for ourselves and asking for help.

Check Up Time With the Radiation Oncologist – A New Type of Radiation? October 24, 2014

It was time for the meeting with the radiation oncologist to see how I was feeling and doing after the 58 radiation treatments. He was pleased with how the skin was repairing after so many treatments. The Vitamin E and Essential Oils that I was using must have been helping. I decided to be completely honest with him and tell him that I felt like I was being "led down the garden path" with the different doctors. At that point, I really felt like I was getting conflicting views from the two different hospitals and what was in my best interest. What I meant by this was that it seemed to me, that despite the agreement on my "diagnosis", there were different opinions between the two hospitals about what to do next. It was obvious to me that they each had my health and best interest as a priority from a medical model standpoint, but things were not clear to me.

As I mentioned before, I really liked this doctor. I felt heard and totally understood by him. After I explained my confusion, he immediately took it upon himself to discuss my situation with their oncologist and surgeon…right then! He actually left the room and made those calls right away. Around fifteen minutes later, he came back in the room with a smile on his face. He reminded me that my case was very individual in that it was unique compared to other patients. He suggested that I meet with another doctor at that same hospital to see if I'm a good candidate for what is called "stereotactic radiosurgery". I was told that stereotactic radiosurgery is a new type of radiation that has a very fine, pin-prick like stream of radiation that goes right into the small lesions of the lung and that it doesn't affect any other organs. This type of treatment was to address the two tiny nodules that were in my lungs. Apparently, this type of surgery was only offered at that particular hospital at that time by a specialist and it had a 99% success rate on small nodules like the ones I had.

This type of treatment was very new and was usually used for patients with brain tumours. He also said they would look at the option of surgery again. He said that after looking at the CT scan, the large lump looked mostly like water and dead cells (necrosis), which was great news! That being said, they couldn't tell for sure without the lump being removed and sent to pathology for testing.

Also, if I chose this procedure, I would have to consider if I should stay in the "out of town lodge" again for another two weeks. The recommended procedure would be done every other day for a total of eight times. It would only take a few minutes each visit and, in fact, it would take longer to set me up then it would to do the actual treatment! He said that despite the fact that I was a very unique case, he felt confident this procedure was a positive step for me to take, if I chose this route.

So now I had to make the choice to have this new kind of radiation surgery or not. As I mentioned, it would mean either travelling for hours every other day, or staying out of town again. I still wanted what was best for **me** and my journey to wellness. After talking to

Steve and a couple friends who also had both the conventional/medical and complementary/holistic therapy backgrounds, I decided I would do it. I would have to wait a couple of weeks for this new form of treatment and would stay at the lodge again to save driving back and forth.

Another Little Bump in the Road... A Broken Foot! November 1, 2014

I was now eleven months into my journey. I was anxiously waiting to begin this new type of radiation I was offered. It would be two weeks before they could get me in to start.

One of our children was moving out to his own basement apartment so Steve and I were going to see his new place. As I walked down the uneven stairs leading to his new abode, I lost my balance and fell over onto my ankle. I felt intense pain at the top of my foot right away. So much so, that I couldn't walk on it in less than a few minutes. Steve and I were off to the hospital the next day. It was still incredibly painful and was swollen and had bruising. I couldn't walk on it if you paid me! Diagnosis: spiral fracture to the long bone in the top of my foot. *Really? Are you freaking kidding me?*

The pain was incredible but considering what I had been through during the last few months, my perception of pain was so much different. I could not believe that after everything I had been through, that this was happening. I now had to deal with a broken foot. Oh, and yes, it was my right foot, which meant that I couldn't drive. *Is the Universe trying to tell me I have to be even more dependent? Am I being directed to ask for even **more** help from those around me?* I wasn't sure about that, but I did have to ask for help.

It was mostly my Dad who drove me everywhere to all my appointments, but friends also came out of the woodwork to help me as well, which made me feel grateful beyond words. The fracture healed very well, despite everything I was going through. I took Arnica Montana, a homeopathic remedy well known for healing injuries and for trauma, to help it heal faster. I also had work done on it by a few of my complementary wellness comrades! I am certain all of these measures helped to heal my foot sooner than it would have otherwise.

Finally, the day came for me to get the new type of radiation. The treatments took two weeks in total. I was living away from home again, but this time with a broken foot. The radiation procedure itself was not painful at all but made me feel very tired. I rested a lot, looked after my broken foot and continued to move forward.

"Life is really simple, but we insist on making it complicated."

— Confucius

What a Great Christmas Gift!
December 17, 2014

Winter was here again. It had been almost a year since I found the ominous lump in my breast. Two weeks before Christmas, I went to get another CT scan to see how things looked after the stereotactic radiosurgery. The results came back six days later, only a week before Christmas. Memories came back to the previous Christmas and all I had been through since then. Steve and I sat in the radiation oncologist's office to await the news. We were nervously awaiting the results, but as always, had a sense of positivity and hope. Yet again, there was still that nervous and daunting feeling of the unknown.

The radiologist walked into the room and happily announced right away that the CT scan showed that the two lesions in the lung were totally gone! Once the appointment was over and he had left the room, Steve and I got up and ran to each other from across the little examination room. It was like a scene from a movie. We hugged each other and cried. I felt my heart racing. I felt joy that is beyond any words I can describe. That was the best Christmas present I could have possibly received. I even called my brother as we walked through the hospital and blurted the news to him, through happy tears, over the phone. *Finally…some positive news.*

<u>Fresh New Year…Fresh New Start</u>

The New Year rang in. I felt so hopeful. It had been more than a year of a very difficult journey. I decided to see Carol, the medical intuitive, again to see if I could get some clarity for the upcoming year. When we got together for my appointment, she told me that she didn't see anything "active" at all in the lump. We discussed that the only way to confirm "no disease" in the medical community is by removing the lump and sending the tissue to pathology for testing. According to both Carol and the radiologist, the lump was "inactive" but at the same time not getting any smaller. Carol said that she would be "amazed" if the lump actually would ever shrink. I found that interesting. But what is more interesting is that she was absolutely right. It never did shrink.

I was questioning continuing taking oral chemotherapy. Half of me was saying *why am I taking any kind of chemotherapy if the scans are coming back looking clear? The other part of me was saying what if I don't take it and therefore it spreads?* We talked about my statements "What if it did or didn't work?" and "What if I didn't do it and because of that decision I may end up dying?" She said that I could choose to actually change my words by saying: **"What if my body could be completely <u>clear</u> of cancer? What if my body is in the best health it could be in and continue to be healthy?"** She said that when the immune system is working well, then it's kind of like "Pac-Man" eating away the cells that may hurt the body. She also said that if you were to give any person, even a healthy person, a scan, they would find abnormal cells somewhere. However, if we have a super healthy immune system, the little "Pac-Men" can find and destroy whatever the body doesn't need. She said that regardless of what I decide in moving forward, that it's important to **embrace** that decision.

She went on to say that one of the worst things a person can do is agree to do something when they really don't **want** to do it. It puts the person into conflict within his or her own body, which can create a totally different outcome. **She said to be at peace with my own decision** - whether I choose to continue oral chemo along with complementary/holistic options, or to just go the holistic route alone. We also talked about recognizing that none of us know what we would do in any particular situation until we are there ourselves and to recognize that anything can work **if we create space for it.**

Will Surgery Ever Happen?

Thirteen months after my diagnosis, my radiation oncologist told me about a friend of his who is a surgeon who specializes in thoracic surgery (surgery in the chest area, with the exception of the heart). Since, at this point, there was no other surgeon willing to take on such a large sized lump, it sounded rather appealing. At this point, the lump was the size of a tennis ball – 15 centimetres (almost 6 inches) in circumference. None of the doctors could figure out why it wasn't getting smaller. Again, it appeared on all the scans to be "stagnant" and "dead cells", but it wasn't shrinking at all.

I am a small-sized person. Not only was this large lump a constant reminder of my situation, but it was very uncomfortable and sore. At times, it actually looked like it was going to push right through the skin. It was daunting. I had to be quite imaginative to even try to hide it under my clothes. Plus there was the mental and psychological component to it. I kept thinking that if I couldn't see it all the time, like if it was deep inside my body, it would be so much easier. The visual of it every single day was a reminder of what I had gone through and the unknown future. I was very aware of it and the thought of it being removed was enough for me to at least book the appointment with this new surgeon.

Surgeon Number Four – Will Surgery Actually Happen This Time? February 13, 2015

I got in to see the thoracic surgeon in less than two weeks. In hindsight, that in itself was a miracle. We all know that there are people who have to wait months to see a specialist! Again, because of the long distance we had to travel, the appointment for the surgeon and the radiation oncologist check up was booked in for the same day.

Steve and I really liked this doctor. He had a kind face and was so calm. He exuded confidence, but no arrogance. I wondered if the lump would be too large for him to remove as I had heard from the other surgeons before him? I liked that this was his **specialty**. It's my experience that this is a very important part of getting advice for what's best for a patient. He had a look at the most recent CT scans and said that all looked good! *What did he say? I hadn't received the recent newest scan results yet…that appointment with the radiation oncologist to get results was later in the day!* Steve and I looked at each other. *Another clear scan? Oh my goodness! This feels like a dream!* We sat quietly smiling at each other.

After examining me, he said again that I was a great candidate for surgery. He even felt that I wouldn't have to have any of my lymph nodes removed! This was a total shock to me. Every other surgeon said that their "standard of care" was usually to remove the lump, the breast that was involved, and the lymph nodes under the armpit that are on the same side as the cancer. He shook our hands and said for me to think about it and, if I was interested in moving forward with the surgery, that he would find me a spot in about three or so weeks.

Steve and I walked out of the hospital like we won the lottery! We were on top of the world with this news! We hugged each other as soon as the doctor left the room. I could feel the happiness in my heart and felt a relief like I've never felt before. *Is this really true? Is this a dream? This is fantastic news!* In the car on our way to the next appointment to see the radiation oncologist, we excitedly talked about the results and about the surgery and finally moving forward. *All is well. Everything is going to be fine.* Or so we thought...

> "Courage is not having the strength to go on; it is going on when you don't have the strength."
>
> — Theodore Roosevelt

Hit By A Train...

Steve and I were giddy with happiness. All the different treatments I was receiving and the effort I was putting in holistically were really working! We walked into the other hospital a couple of hours later like two little school age children. We sat down in the office for another waiting game. At that point, we didn't care. We were celebrating tonight! The radiologist walked in with his assistant and asked how I was. I shared my happy story with him and that the possibility of surgery was back on the table. I thanked him for the great referral to this new surgeon and told him I was looking forward to making a date for surgery. But as I was speaking, I felt that he looked at me in a strange, concerned way. Right after I stopped talking, he said he would be back shortly. He left the room. *That's strange. What's going on?*

About twenty minutes later, he came back into the room. He looked concerned; somber. He went on to tell us that he just had his own specialists and radiologists look at my scan much closer (than the thoracic surgeon would). They were concerned because there "appeared" to be more lesions on my lungs. They didn't feel that surgery was in my best interest, but rather suggested I do chemotherapy again. I'm sure he could see that I clearly looked shocked. Again, I couldn't look at Steve. *What the hell? Why is this happening? Is this just a really bad joke? How can we go from a state of bliss to a state of horror in a matter of hours? What about all the work I've done? What about all the effort I've put in? What about all the treatments? What about what the thoracic surgeon said?*

He said he was genuinely sorry to have to share this news with me, and that his team of radiologists were very specialized in picking up this kind of thing on a scan. Clearly he could see I looked defeated. In hindsight I can't imagine doing his job. It must be tough to see the reaction on different patients' faces after delivering that kind of news. He suggested I go back to my hometown oncologist to start treatments as soon as possible. Steve and I quietly sat there after he left. We didn't look at each other. We just sat there, stunned. I got up first and said, "let's get out of here".

At that point, I could have thrown up my arms in defeat. I was tired. I had been through the darkest times in my life with so much positivity and was feeling flat and defeated. This was almost too much, even for me. On the long ride home, Steve and I discussed the recent news. It was a shock to say the least, but I dug inside myself and felt a little "knowing" inside of me that told me I would still be okay. I could hear *don't give up now, Jill. It's going to be okay. Keep trusting your intuition and just do what you need to do.* That little voice was what kept me going.

Steve and I decided that we would "edit" this new information when we had to share how my appointment went. After all the positive work I had done, the last thing I wanted was for people who loved me to get alarmed or concerned. My strong belief and intuition kept telling me that sharing the details with everyone wouldn't be in my best interest. I was very strong in my belief that I needed to keep surrounding myself with only positive energy. Plus, I kept reminding myself that scans are not always the true measure of what is really happening in your body; that the only way to truly prove a person has cancer is to do a pathology test on it; that I still had control of my choices.

Taken from my "emotional journal" the day after I found out the surgery was cancelled yet again: "Wow...roller coaster ride supreme! Surgery was cancelled again. At first I flipped out, and went to a dark place feeling out of control and felt hopeless. But, I just have to dust myself off and get back in the ring! Lol Well, actually it would be better put: I have acceptance and peaceful thoughts about the next steps, knowing that I will be fine. I'm so healthy and strong and my body can handle this next hurdle. I'm staying positive about it, nonetheless. One day at a time, Jill...one day at a time."

I could have made the choice to say that my situation was getting worse, but my solid belief of energy far outweighed that option. With all the books I have read and the research I have personally done, I truly believe in the power of energy and thoughts. There are many books that talk about this. Some of my favourite authors are: Dr. Wayne Dyer, Deepak Chopra, Doreen Virtue, Eckhart Tolle and Louise Hay. There are hundreds of incredible authors and books and information about this concept out there, and I can tell hundreds of stories on how it can alter a person's life in a positive way.

My Decision

I decided after much contemplating, discussions with a very few of my holistic practitioners, and a meeting with my "at home" oncologist, that I would start intravenous chemotherapy again. This time, the dose would be less because of the stress it puts on the heart. I probably would lose my hair again, which was finally growing in to a pixie cut. At this point, that was the least of my concerns. I also decided I was going to continue on with all my complementary and holistic approaches. I wanted to keep my body strong during this time.

Cancer, A Broken Foot... Let's Add In Pneumonia – March 8, 2015

I started the chemo treatments again. This time I wasn't the rookie. I decided I would still do my usual visualizations while getting the dose put into my veins. *This medicine is healing me. It's doing its job. I am well. Every cell is getting healthier and healthier.* I still listened to my calm music and meditated during the treatments. I still visualized my body being completely healthy and having the power to heal itself. *I am getting through this.*

I already knew that one of the side effects of chemotherapy was that the immune system gets compromised. That's one of the reasons the doctors order blood work before a cancer patient gets each of their treatments. The doctors are actually making sure the patient's body is strong enough to handle the drug(s). A few days after I started the new round of chemo, I started feeling really rough. It felt like I was getting a chest cold. It was the weekend after I started receiving treatments and I was feeling so poorly that Steve took me to the hospital to get my lungs checked. I felt really sick. I could barely breathe. *I was scared.*

We decided to go to the emergency at the local hospital where I was receiving my chemo treatments. Even though it was a Sunday, the emergency doctor(s) would have my charts there. Steve wheeled me into the emergency room in a wheelchair. At that point, I wasn't even strong enough to walk. It felt like eternity waiting to be checked. Eventually, it was my turn and the doctor listened to my chest. At one point I was coughing so hard that it made me vomit. A chest x-ray was ordered and I had to wait for the doctor to get results.

I sat slumped in a very uncomfortable chair, feeling like I could barely breathe, feeling the effects of the recent chemo treatment and coughing convulsively. I knew Steve was really worried about me. *I could just feel it.* I was at the hospital emergency department for a total of eight hours. When I felt like I couldn't stay there another second, the doctor finally came over to me. It turns out she was the only doctor working that day in emergency. She said that I had pneumonia, told me it could take weeks to get better, gave me a prescription for antibiotics and sent me on my way. I was happy to be leaving, knowing my comfortable bed wasn't far away. Steve wheeled me back to the car. It wasn't long before we were home.

I had found out that it usually takes weeks to months for a person with pneumonia to get well again. A person with pneumonia is very weak, very tired and can be coughing on an off. It can get very serious, very fast. It's the most tired I have ever felt. I barely had the energy to get to the washroom. Walking up stairs just wasn't an option, never mind the thought of walking my dog on the trails or doing yoga. My bed became my new home. For the moment, chemo treatments were brought to a halt. I was way too sick to receive treatments.

While lying in my bed, feeling like death warmed over, I slept a lot for the first few days. I was praying that the antibiotics would kick in and I would start feeling better. After the third day, I was feeling a bit better. I was still very weak and tired. Intermittently, when I felt up to it, I was still meditating and doing visualizations on being well. On that third day, I had a thought: *I'm sure there must be holistic options to help pneumonia. I need to find that out!* I weakly called a few of my holistic practitioner friends and then started taking Oil of Oregano. I also kept visualizing that I was getting better. One week after that hospital visit, I was up and feeling better. At **day nine**, I was checked by my GP and the pneumonia was **gone**! My body was strong and nothing was going to pull me down.

An Appointment to Visit "The Angel Lady" – Maria Del Carmen Orlandis-Habsburgo, Baroness of Pinopar – March 14, 2015

Carmen (or "YaYa", which means grandmother, as she is referred) is a spiritual and ritual coach that my friend, Simone, invited me to experience. Carmen is a very interesting lady. She had such a beautiful energy that made you feel like you have known her forever. Her beautiful accent and warm energy immediately captivated our hearts and we were all open to the experience.

My friends Simone, Katie, Janel, Heather and I went to see her as a gift from Simone. She had purchased Carmen's donation called "The Archangel Raphael Experience" at the on-line fundraiser and wanted to see what it was all about as well! The time with my friends at Carmen's was like nothing I have ever experienced. This beautiful lady knew more about angels and history than anyone I have ever met. She had us all captivated with her teachings and ceremonies that she gently and lovingly carried out with us. My knowledge was expanded to what was offered from this new perspective and I did go back to her another two times. It was a fascinating experience and again, all part of my interesting journey! I know this may sound out of the box for so many people, but it was something I don't regret. I called on angels many times in my journey, especially when I was feeling scared or at my wits end. It seemed to help quite significantly.

New Round of Chemo Was Two-Thirds Complete / Another Scan is Ordered – April 30, 2015

It was now sixteen months after that telephone call with the news that my life would never be the same again. I was back on chemo again now that I was feeling better and the pneumonia was gone. I was back at my oncologist's office for my pre-chemo blood work and check up. I was two-thirds of the way through the new round of chemo treatments. I told her that I had an upcoming appointment with the thoracic surgeon in the next few weeks and that I really wanted to have the lump removed. It was incredibly uncomfortable. It could be seen through my clothing… I felt it was ready to go. As I mentioned, it was the size of a tennis ball.

Despite the results showing it most likely was just dead cells, it was that constant reminder of what might be. I remember meditating one day and feeling like the lump had "taught" me all it needed to and that it was time for it to go. In the appointment, I also shared with the oncologist that almost two years prior Steve, my dad and I had booked travel to the United Kingdom to visit family in the next few weeks. My dad's brother and family live in Jersey in the Channel Islands and we all were very much looking forward to this holiday. I really wanted to go on this trip. Since we were already booked to go away, she actually said that it might be a good time to give my body a break. She said it wasn't uncommon for patients to take a break from chemo, especially if they want to travel. She recommended getting another CT scan before I left, though, to see where I was at. I was so relieved that she supported my desire to not have to cancel my trip again. We had previously rescheduled the trip in the fall when I had chose to receive stereotactic radiation treatments for my lungs.

The days closed in to the time we were leaving to visit our United Kingdom family. I was so excited about going away and seeing everyone. The scan results hadn't come back yet. To be completely honest I wasn't sure that I wanted to hear the results before we left. *If all was clear, we can celebrate while we're away. But if it's anything other than that… ugh.*

It was the day before our holiday. Between resting when I my body felt tired, getting another couple of chemo treatments, ongoing holistic appointments, and gentle yoga and meditating, I was getting excited about going away. It felt great that I could go away with two of the closest people in my life, dad and Steve, to visit my dad's family. If I was tired, I could just lay down. If I felt unwell, they would be there to help me. I was so looking forward to just getting away from it all and seeing more of my family. My curiosity took the better of me, and I decided to call my oncologist's office to see if the results had come back. I heard her voice on the line and she told me that she had been checking for the results, but at the last check, they were not in. She then actually asked me if I wanted to know the results before I left for vacation. She knew me well enough to know how stressed out I could get when waiting for results. I really respected her for that. *She was thinking about her patient in a very sensitive and deep way. She knew me well and was giving me that option.*

They say that "curiosity killed the cat". That may be true because I told her that I **did** want to hear the results. I could hear her clicking away on her computer. She said that the results had just come in. I waited to hear what she had to say. I was in my bedroom, laying on my bed and staring at the ceiling… almost holding my breath. She said that the bone scan looked clear. *Awesome!* Silence on the phone. She then said that it was hard to tell, but it looked like one of the lesions may be getting bigger. *What? Breathe, Jill… Breathe. Remember you have the choice how to take this news. You don't have to buy in. There are always options.*

She hesitated for what felt like the longest time. She went on to say that it was interesting that despite what the scan showed, all my tumour markers were clear. This was astonishing. Tumour markers are one of the guidelines for doctors to track patients with cancer. My understanding is that they aren't used by all doctors and hospitals. *This was a positive sign. If the tumour markers are showing clear, then **that** is what I'm holding on to. My blood is showing I am healthy, so I* *am going to focus on that.* All I needed was this small little "light" - a little ray of more hope to grab on to. She suggested that I just go on my holiday and try not to think about anything but having a great time and connect with family. I was taking a break from chemo and I was going to enjoy myself, stay in the moment, and enjoy the vacation as best as I could.

My dad, Steve and I had a spectacular time away. We were there for just over two weeks. We enjoyed visiting our family and feeling the love around us. I rested when I needed to. We enjoyed the sites and each other's company when I was strong enough to do so. It felt very healing. It was a little refuge away from all the appointments, the hospitals, the doctors and the treatments. I did have thoughts about what was ahead of me when I returned. I thought about the phone call I had with my oncologist before we left. I thought about what my options could be in my future. That being said, I made a sincere effort to enjoy each and every moment while we were away.

I also knew that if I was going to choose to have surgery, chemo a few weeks before and after would be off the table. With cancer patients, chemo has to stop a few weeks before and after surgery. In the oncology model, a patient has to be off chemo because they have to be strong enough to handle the assault on the body, that being the surgery. With this knowledge, I made a decision. When I returned, I would ask my naturopath that since I knew I wasn't going to be on chemo for quite some time, what could I take to help support my body from a holistic standpoint that would take the place of chemo? Of course, while I was away on vacation, I meditated every day and kept taking my holistic and homeopathic remedies that I was on at the time.

"Our greatest glory is not in never falling, but in rising every time we fall."

— Confucius

Back to the Thoracic Surgeon – May 22, 2015

The day after we returned back from our holiday, Steve and I drove to the "out of town" hospital to see the thoracic surgeon again. *What would he say about moving forward with surgery?* Despite my wanting to have the lump removed, I wasn't sure where he would stand in operating due to the most recent scan results. His warm smile and energy filled the room when he walked in and his pleasant, quiet presence could immediately be felt.

He examined me and said that if I did choose to have surgery, he most likely would only have to remove the lump alone, since it seemed to be encapsulated and not involving any muscle or ribs. However, there was a small possibility that once he started operating and could therefore see inside, he might have to take out muscle, ribs or even the lymph nodes under the armpit. For that reason, he would want to book me into the intensive care unit (ICU) after surgery, just in case. I would have to sign papers for a possible blood transfusion if that was the case as well. Again, he said he didn't think it would be necessary to take out the lymph nodes.

He pointed out the most recent radiologist report about the lungs, but said he could understand why I would want this large mass removed. He understood how it could be getting in the way and even psychologically how having this "reminder" every day would be difficult. *I like that he is recognizing that. He was very tuned in to his patient and seemed to really care.*

If I still wanted to move forward with surgery, he had an opening in a couple weeks. It may be a complicated surgery, but either way I was to expect to be in the hospital at least four to five days. I didn't hesitate. *It's time. It feels right. It's been a long, rough road and it's time for this lump to leave my body.* We left the office, went through the pre-operation screening and procedure while we were there, and headed for the long drive home. *I wonder if surgery will actually go through this time?*

I would be lying if I said in the next twelve days I hadn't wondered many times if the surgery would be cancelled. May I remind you that over the last 17 months, surgery had been put on the table and then cancelled **three times!** One time it was cancelled **six days** before the surgery was to happen! But now, I was in a different space. I was learning to trust more. I was learning to settle into "being in the moment". If this surgery was meant to be, it would happen. I was learning to be more at peace with whatever came my way. *This feeling was empowering.*

Two days before the surgery date, I went to see my naturopath. If surgery was going to happen, I wanted to support my body as much as possible to make the surgery as successful as possible. As I mentioned with the broken foot, I knew that one of the best-kept secrets out there was to take the homeopathic remedy called Arnica Montana before and after surgery, which has been known to speed up healing. I also knew that anesthetic was very hard on the body, especially to the liver and kidneys, so once surgery was completed I would get holistic treatments done and get support that would help clear my body of the drugs…if indeed the surgery was going to go through!

Surgery Was Really Happening – June 3, 2015

It had now been 18 months since my diagnosis. The night before surgery, Steve and I stayed close to the hospital at our good friend Rob's, apartment. Surgery was booked for early in the day. Staying at Rob's would alleviate the stress of a possible two to three hour "rush hour traffic" drive! It indeed was a blessing and we were very grateful that he offered his place to us.

The alarm clock rang. *Surgery day?* At this point, I was **still** questioning whether it really was going to carry through. We got in the car and headed on the ten-minute journey to the hospital. I was very excited but also very nervous. We all have heard those stories about the surgeon opening someone up, finding the situation is much worse than they thought, and then sewing them back up again. It may sound dramatic, but that thought **did** actually cross my mind. *After all, I'm human.* But that was where the power of thoughts came in. I did think the thought, but then right after that I made a choice to replace it with thoughts of a great outcome; thoughts of the surgery going smoothly; thoughts that all the surgeon would have to do is remove the lump and everything would go well. I was feeling very hopeful. I was living in the moment.

As they wheeled me into the operating room, I thought *this is really happening. The surgery is actually really going to happen!* I admitted to the doctor that I was feeling quite nervous. He reassured me. I remember the last face I saw when I fell asleep under the anesthetic. It was the warm, kind face of the thoracic surgeon.

As I came to in the recovery room, the first blurry vision I saw was a clock on the wall. It was not long after twelve noon. *It's done. The surgery is done.* As I came in and out of consciousness, I wondered what the outcome was. *Did he have to cut out muscle or ribs? Did he have to take the lymph nodes after all? What was actually done?* What was so interesting is that, although it was hard to explain, I felt somehow different. I felt a sense of peace that I hadn't recalled before; like I had been looked after…like there was some kind of "shift".

As the scenes around me became more and more clear, I could see the hustle and bustle of the nurses coming and going. I looked down and with a sigh noticed that my large, tennis ball-sized passenger was gone. I slowly lifted up the hospital gown and saw the bright, white bandages covering a small area. *He didn't have to take the lymph nodes! That's a great sign.* I saw that there was only one drainage port, which was another good sign. Under the bandages it was flat. *For so long I carried that bump around with me, and now it was gone. What a surreal feeling.*

The surgeon was the first person who I remember talking to after surgery. He stood at my side and even through my drugged-up stupor, I heard him loud and clear. The surgery had gone very well. It took a lot less time than he had anticipated. He just had to remove the lump and stretch/pull some muscle and skin over, like he had thought. I'm not even sure if he said anything after that. I was just feeling elated that it was a less complicated surgery than expected and that the "passenger" was gone.

Poor Steve was pacing in the waiting room for almost two hours after the surgery was done but finally he was by my side in the recovery room. Despite the surgery going so well with no complications, they wanted to keep a close watch on me in the ICU.

I Surprised the Doctors and Nurses

By the time I left the recovery room, I was totally aware of everything around me. I actually felt really great! *I feel lighter. Is that possible?* The intern wheeled me through the hospital on a gurney. I was taken from recovery to a small room in the ICU. After they maneuvered the large moving bed through the doors, there was the task of getting me over to the bed waiting for me in the room. There were about three or four interns and nurses squished into the room that now had two beds in it – the gurney and the hospital bed. They were all discussing how to best move me over to the other bed. I thought: *I can just move over there myself. Is that weird that I think I can do that? I know my body…I feel strong enough to do that!* So I did.

I gently sat up and wiggled myself over to the awaiting bed. I honestly didn't think anything of it, but it created quite the reaction. Their faces were actually quite amusing. They all had a look of shock and were making comments about how incredible it was that I could do that. *Weird…it was not **that** difficult.* The room cleared out. One nurse remained that had been assigned to me while I stayed in the ICU. He was really nice. He came in many times for the first few hours and during the night. They were watching me closely.

That night was a very long night. I had my "pain medication button" right beside me, but I only used it a few times. I actually felt really good. My sleep was interrupted constantly with different nurses checking my blood pressure and heart rate. During the night, I told the nurse I was well enough to walk to the washroom, which was in the same room, about five feet away from my bed. I got a puzzled-looking face after I said that, but I did just that – I checked in to see how my body felt and very slowly and carefully got myself to the washroom with the nurse close beside me.

Throughout the night, I could hear different monitors, intermittent commotion in the hallways, and the sound of moaning. It's a sound I will never forget. It was the sound of people in pain…people most likely suffering. It was daunting. I remember wondering *why am I in the ICU? I feel so blessed that I feel so good. Those poor people. I wonder what their situation is?*

Although I thought the night would never end, it did. That morning, the pleasant male nurse was making jokes with me that looking after me was "boring" because I was such an easy patient, and I was doing so well! He told me that my blood work looked great. In fact, he said it was "extraordinary". My first thought when he said that was *that's because I have supported my body with holistic measures. It has to be!* The surgeon came in to see me. He was impressed with how well I was doing…so impressed that he said I could go home in a few hours! *A few hours? What happened to "you'll be staying in the*

ICU for the first day or two and should be out of the hospital in four to five days?" This was incredible!

I was so happy at the thought of being home and in my own bed, where it was quiet and had great, healing energy. I would be away from the beeps of the machines and all the sounds. The nurse came back in and said he wasn't surprised I was being released. He shared with me that he has worked in that hospital for over ten years. He went on to share with me that in ten years, I was only the third patient released from ICU within 24 hours. *Wow. The power of taking care of your body. The power of the mind. Love it!*

Post Surgery – Check up by the Thoracic Surgeon – June 15, 2015

My post surgery appointment was two weeks after the operation. Despite the long drive, I was looking forward to seeing my surgeon. After the examination, he said that the wound was looking great and healing fantastically. I was not surprised by his words. I had a great surgeon, I had been taking Arnica, I was looking after the wound with Vitamin E and essential oils, and I was supporting my body on the inside with supplements. Again, I was doing as much as I could to support the healing of my body.

Colon Hydrotherapy

While healing after surgery, my reflexologist friend, Joanne Trumper told me about a practitioner she recommended in Oakville. Joanne was reminding me about the importance of de-toxing the body after treatments like chemotherapy or after anesthetic from surgery. Despite the fact that drugs can help people, they can take a toll on the body, particularly the liver and the kidneys, which are responsible for filtering out what your body doesn't need. She was telling me about a technique called "colon hydrotherapy." For the readers that don't know what this is, it may conjure up quite the interesting visuals!

What I will tell you, though, is that despite whether you have cancer or any other condition, digestive health and keeping the colon clean is of paramount importance. I have learned that having a healthy colon and intestinal track is much more important that one would think. Maureen McLaughlin is a phenomenal colon hydrotherapy practitioner. What could be a very uncomfortable, intimidating procedure is far from that with her. She will tell you her fascinating story of how she believes it saved her life. For an excellent video about this type of treatment, go to:

https://www.youtube.com/watch?v=0AXHD5H9nEQ

This fifteen minute, well done, fantastic video will help clarify why this is so important for your health. I saw Maureen quite regularly for a couple months, and now I go every couple of months for "maintenance". I look at it like getting an oil change and tune up on your car, like I mentioned earlier. If you buy a car and don't do anything at all to maintain it, you would be up against a totally different scenario than if you did the recommended maintenance schedule. Like a car, with maintenance your body runs smoother and is healthier!

"Wherever you go, go with all your heart."

— Confucius

Came Clean With my Oncologist – July 3, 2015

While healing from surgery and waiting for my next oncology appointment, I carried on seeing all the practitioners for holistic treatments and taking all my remedies. A month after surgery,

Steve and I showed up at my appointment. It was great to see my oncologist. She had been a large part of my journey and I felt a closeness to her that is difficult to explain. I told her that since the last time I saw her, I made the decision to support myself with full time holistic care. I explained that since I wasn't on any kind of chemo for such a long time, I wanted to do something holistic to support my body before and after surgery. I wasn't sure how she would react to my honesty. I totally understand that cancer doctors can only give you advice, suggestions and support on what is in their own tool pouch of knowledge. I also understand that, from their perspective, there was no solid proof that any of what I was doing would actually work.

She was very supportive, as usual, of my decision. I figured that it must be awkward for her. I understood that she could only offer me what was in the "oncology box" of cancer care. She then asked me if I wanted to get another CT scan to see how I was doing. That question made me stop in my tracks. *She's asking me if I want one?* Apparently, there are two reasons patients in my scenario get scans done: one - if they request it for a medical perspective of their condition, but mostly two - to help the oncologists make a decision of what chemo would be best for the patient, depending on where the cancer was located.

I found that one of the worst things about having cancer is the feeling of not being in control. Waiting for results was, to put it mildly, stressful. So I said to her that I would think about it, and she said all I had to do was call and she would order the scan right away for me. We agreed that she would see me in another four weeks to discuss how I was feeling and check my blood and tumour markers again. If I had any concerns or symptoms that worried me, she was only a phone call away. She let me know that my blood tests looked great and the markers were clear again! This was a very big day for me. It felt like it was a turning point.

I went home and had to really think about our conversation. Since I had decided to go ahead with surgery, I hadn't been on chemo for over twelve weeks! I talked to Steve about it, got feedback from my holistic practitioners, and meditated and prayed about it. Finally, one day I had what I feel was another epiphany. I thought to myself: *If I do go and get a scan done now, one of three things will come back in those results. I will be sitting in the doctor's office hearing: One – everything looks clear. We don't know why, but your scans are all clear! It's a miracle! Or two – things look the same as in the last scan...so now what? Or three – it "appears" as if the cancer is in more organs now. Again, so now what do I do?*

After all I had been through: the symptoms, the pain, the treatments, the surgery, the roller coaster ride of events and emotions, the tiredness, the stress, the worry… I had come to a place of acceptance and trust. I had come to a place that regardless of what the scans may show, I didn't think I would do chemo or radiation again. It's not that I regret doing conventional treatments. In fact, I believe that they had a very important part in saving my life. But I just was not prepared to go down that road again **at this point**.

I was feeling so great and healthy, getting back to feeling like myself (but a new version!), and wanting to move forward in my life with the mindset that *I am well and have a perfectly healthy body.* There was nothing that could argue with that at this point. I didn't want something read as "suspicious" on a scan to alter that thought process. I knew I could always change my mind, but for now, that is what felt right to me. It was my choice. It was freeing to feel that. It was freeing to realize that I had control of what I was going to do, and that was to carry on in my life in the healthy body that I knew I had. That doesn't mean that fear could never come along and rear its ugly head again…

"If you are depressed, you are living in the *past*. If you are anxious, you are living in the *future*. If you are at peace, you are living in the present."

— Lao Tzu

Chest Pain... What's This About?

I was continuing with all my holistic approaches, homeopathy and supplements during the weeks after my surgery. I also continued on with my meditation as well as yoga and walking my dog when I felt up to it. The healing was going well and my energy levels were getting better. I still had to rest and if I did too much, I would be knocked off my feet - sometimes for a day or two.

As the weeks progressed, I started feeling discomfort and pain under my surgery site. Despite all the work I had done over the last year and a half, I still had my moments of fear. *What if that pain is cancer and not just from the body healing from surgery? Could it be?* Taken from my "emotional journal" at that time: *"Feeling really negative today. I have pain in my right chest that haunts me. I'm questioning everything again. I wonder how long this pain will go and of course I question exactly "what" it is. I wonder if I should get a CT scan? But if I do, then what? Sublime to ridiculous enters my mind. It can be literally maddening and crazy making. How simple life used to be ... living in ignorant bliss...thinking you're in control when maybe you really are not. I try living in the moment, but my crazy thoughts get to me lately. The emotional roller coaster is EXHAUSTING... Time to meditate."*

Apparently, this way of thinking is very normal for cancer patients and survivors. Any little pain or twinge can bring them back to that place of fear; back to the place of questioning what is happening in their body. The mind can play tricks on a person. This is when the importance of choice comes in. The fact is that, as humans, we actually get to make choices in our life. This is something most people seem to forget. I considered the thought of requesting a scan, but my intuition kept saying that it wasn't the time, at least not just yet. Since I had the awareness of having a choice, I decided to go to a few different holistic practitioners first to see if their treatments would alleviate the pain. If the pain didn't go away, I would go back to the doctors and have it checked out. I felt like I was being a responsible patient and not allowing myself to be run by fear.

The first place I went was to my friend Simone. She is the great friend that joined me at a few of my appointments; the one who worked in the cancer centre as an x-ray technician and also had a holistic background. I thought that she would be the best place to start, since she has the background knowledge in cancer care and would help me to be subjective about the pains I was having. Simone has a way of listening to what a client has to say, reframing and explaining the options the client thinks they have, and then she helps clarify the choices.

She's a great teacher to guide people to **check in with themselves** and explore what is possible at any given moment. When something shows up in our lives, there's never just one option. I remember her saying that "it's like pulling apart a ball of yarn to see all the pieces you have in front of you". I knew she would receive the news of the pain in my chest, and my thoughts and choices surrounding it, in a neutral non-judgmental way. She worked around the surgery site and did some treatments from "The One Command®" with me. The next day I felt a lot better. The pain was less.

I also decided to see my Shiatsu therapist and dear friend Ann as well for the pain. Her calm, caring, warm personality and intense expertise with Shiatsu also helped tremendously. She would not only work on the site around the surgery and radiation, but would make sure the rest of my body was balanced and looked after. It's a lot of work recovering from all the treatments my body endured over almost two years! I also made sure to see her husband, Dave Tysdale, who is a chiropractor . Sometimes, when a person has surgery, the ribs can get "popped" out of place and if you've ever had a rib out, it's painful! I call him the "rib specialist" because he has helped many patients with rib issues. Dave helped me a number of times as well and each time the pain was less and I felt better.

Finally, regarding the pain in my chest, I made a choice to see my osteopath Norm Hatch . I only saw him a few times, but his treatments always helped me and the pain would always decrease after a treatment.

In the few weeks of my journey of dealing with the chest pain, and making the choice to go for these four different types of treatments, I learned a common "thread" with **all** of them. After any kind of surgery, it is very common to have lingering pain to various degrees, sometimes for years! Some of the reasons for this pain are possible nerve damage, scar tissue, and the connective tissues and fascia all trying to compensate after surgery. Needless to say, the pain went down tremendously with all their help. That being said, if I did too much and over exerted myself, the pain would get worse.

As I sit writing the book, for the most part the pain has totally gone from my chest. If I do too much, it does come back, but with **much** less intensity. And yes, I will continue to be supported by my holistic practitioners as I move forward in my journey of wellness. I believe that each of these practitioners helped the pain in my chest get so much better. Other than seeing them, I changed nothing.

> "Happiness does not depend on what you have or who you are. It solely relies on what you think."
>
> — Buddha

Another Epiphany – August 19, 2015

Now, it had been almost twenty months since I found the lump in my breast. I had been through so much. My body and mind had been through the wringer! It was quite literally a roller coaster ride that I would never forget. It was rapidly changing my life.

I went to see my naturopath, Melissa Howe once again, to discuss my moving forward. I was still getting different holistic treatments and taking remedies and supplements to support my body. My oncologist was seeing me every four to six weeks. The tumor markers were showing clear every time. Meditation and yoga were two of my closest friends. We talked about all the choices that led me to that day. After that visit and our discussion together, I had another epiphany: **It was time to really move forward with the mindset as a "survivor" and a healthy person.**

As I have mentioned, the power of the mind is incredible. I believe that our thoughts are more powerful than we give them credit for. A perfect example is a story I heard in the CD set: "There is a Spiritual Solution to Every Problem" by Dr. Wayne Dyer. It's a six CD set of a live lecture he did back in the early 2000's. Written by one of my favourite teachers in my life, Dr. Dyer talks about a story he heard about a physician who hadn't been for a physical examination in 25 years. He had to go in to have a physical for a life insurance requirement. They took an x-ray and found a big black mark on his lung. They told him he had lung cancer. Sadly, four months later he died. After his death, a friend of his was cleaning out the physician's office and going through his things. He came across an x-ray from 25 years previous when the physician first entered medical school. There it was… the same big black mark. He had it for 25 years, but the moment he found out about it he was gone in four months. Coincidence? Perhaps. But I wonder how is it that he carried that around for more than two decades, but once he found out about it, he passed away. What **is** that about? Is this a perfect example of how strong and powerful our thoughts are? I believe so.

I had made many choices, but the main choices were to embrace conventional and holistic treatments **together**, learn to trust myself and the choices I was making, and to learn more about Jill and what would help her heal. I don't regret anything I did. I believe it was all in perfect order and everything I chose to do was an integral part of saving my life, and why I'm still on the planet.

My choice to not get scans done (to this date) meant I have never "officially" got a "you're cancer free" (or at least in remission) from the medical community. Again, that was my **choice**. I made a choice that I wasn't going to live in fear and attach myself to "what may be" but rather live in the moment, eat responsibly, meditate daily, keep up with yoga and exercise, and be aware of my thoughts. Most of all… take care of Jill on every level. I do all of this with the knowledge that I have choices and can change my mind at any given moment.

Not So Naïve

I'm not writing this book believing that things for me may not change on a dime. That would be naïve. It would also be unrealistic. I believe the choices that I made have brought me to where I am today. I am feeling wonderful and strong. I am still taking remedies and getting treatments from my holistic health care practitioners to this day on a regular basis. I am more in the moment. I look and feel very well. I keep telling myself that I am well and that I have a perfectly healthy body. We all know that could change in a heartbeat. That being said, it is most important to note that this is the same for **anyone**. Any one of us could live for one more minute or live for many more years. One fact that can't be argued is that we are all going to die. We are born on this planet, and we will die on this planet. None of us knows when that day will be. We don't have a crystal ball to tell us this. It's still a fact.

The difference between my story and many is that I made a choice to explore my options, ask for help, receive it graciously and with appreciation, live in the moment, enjoy life to the fullest, appreciate all I have, be aware of my thoughts, and be grateful that I have a healthy body and I have choices at any given moment in my life.

"Do not dwell in the past, do not dream of the future,
concentrate the mind on the present moment."

— Buddha

Synopsis

During the last two years of this "journey" I've been on, there were times that I actually would have liked to go back to the past in a time machine. I wish I could prove why **exactly** I am living today. But with that being said, I strongly believe that everything happens in the perfect time it is supposed to happen. If you learn to stay aware and take the time to observe when something is being presented to you, it could possibly change your life forever.

The fact that you are reading this book indicates to me that you could be ready to move forward in your life to change this present moment to a healthier one. "Healthier" doesn't necessarily mean physically but can mean mentally, emotionally and spiritually as well. Nevertheless, whether we live to be one minute old or 101 years old, we are living on this planet for a finite amount of time. How we choose to live those minutes, days, weeks, months or years, is entirely up to each of us and the choices we make. What is beautiful about this statement is that it all really boils down to "choice". Regardless of what people tell you, the bottom line is that you get to choose what to do next. This can be an empowering thought or a terrifying one. Think about it… You choose everything in your life. You can choose to listen or not to listen. You can choose to take a particular piece of advice or not. Which leads me to remind you of an important point – you can even choose what you think about. It's true. Your mind is indeed yours. Every single piece of information, regardless of where it came from, all starts in your mind. Knowing you have control over those thoughts can be daunting for sure, but the truth is that it is actually very empowering.

As I mentioned earlier in the book, one of my favourite authors, Dr. Wayne Dyer, talked about this subject quite often. He has authored many books on the power of our thoughts and intention. He is actually the first person who helped me turn my life around to a place of awareness. For that, I am eternally grateful. I never actually knew Dr. Dyer, but I **felt** like I did. He was a beautiful soul on our planet who helped change the lives of literally millions of people as he went through his own journey. I've read many of his books, but as I mentioned, one of my favourites is, "There is a Spiritual Solution to Every Problem". Now don't let the word "spiritual" scare or intimidate you. Regardless of whether you believe in God, Jesus, Allah, Krishna, Buddha, Source, The Universe, The Creator, the God within you, or a combination of all of them… it doesn't really matter. What does matter is that regardless of what you believe from a spiritual perspective, I believe it can help you get through **anything**. It's one of the important pieces of the human existence and in healing us in our journey on planet Earth.

Is it Possible to Know How a Person Gets Cancer?

Throughout the almost two years of my journey, the question has been asked frequently: "how do you think you got cancer?" For me, the answer to that question is unclear. Some may say it was genetic, since my mother and grandmother both had breast cancer. That being said, when I had the intensive genetic testing done, as mentioned earlier in the book, I found out that it surprisingly came back negative! I remember getting the call from the genetic testing office with the results. I was so happy to receive the "negative" results, since it meant that the cancer most likely wasn't being carried genetically within me. My daughter, Lindsey, and I danced in the kitchen that day! As a mother, I was indeed relieved.

So how, or should I ask why, did cancer come knocking on my door? Was it my diet, stress, the foods I was eating, the pollution in the air? Was my immune system simply compromised or as some may say, "it was just plain bad luck"? To this day, there is nothing to actually **prove** how I got this disease.

However, after all I have gone through, and all I have learned over the years, it's my opinion that there may be at least two factors that contributed to it showing up in my life. One of them most likely won't come as a surprise – stress…that simple, yet powerful six-letter word. Now you might be saying that everyone has stress on many different levels! I believe that to be very true. But I don't think it's the actual stress that causes a "dis-ease" in the body, but more importantly how a person **handles** the stress that comes into their life. It doesn't matter who you are, your set of circumstances, the continent you live in, the culture you come from… stress is inevitable.

Perception of stress is very subjective. A four-month old baby could be stressed because they are hungry. A student could be stressed about life and exams. A parent could be stressed about their child's wellbeing. A couple could be fretting about finances, or a woman in a retirement home could be stressed about which colour of yarn should go into the next project. The point is that, for the most part, stress cannot be avoided in life. That being said, it's my experience that if you handle the stress coming your way in a healthy manner, your body, mind and soul can only benefit. That's where self-care and asking for help comes in. That's when things like meditation, yoga, or anything to support you and your body and finding ways to decrease your stress comes in.

The importance of this is so hard to convey, even in words. I can tell you that I believe **how I handled my stress** was key. In the early days, I didn't do this very well and I believe it may have been a major contributor to my illness. Many times I would push my true emotions down and "put on a happy face" like everything was always okay, even when I was sad or angry. As part of my learning process, I practiced recognizing and being honest with how I felt when I was feeling stress. After the awareness of **knowing** I was stressed, I went to what I call "my tool pouch of choices". I had to manage the stress. For example, I changed a negative thought to a positive one, which only takes a heartbeat in time! Alternatively, I stopped whatever I was doing, if possible, to meditate or do yoga. Obviously, sometimes this had to wait until I had the time later in the day. I talked to Steve, friends, professionals or colleagues. I read an inspirational poem or book. Or I did something just for **me**.

The second reason I believe cancer came into my life may sound very strange to many people. When I first found out, as I mentioned, I was angry, scared and totally feeling the "victim" role. As you would imagine, that would be a common response to such news. Now that I have learned what I have learned and gotten to the place I am in my life, I believe that it may have been actually… a blessing. *I can hear the gasps. I can see the puzzled faces. Perhaps there is confusion. Maybe even judgement.* Let me explain: I call it a blessing because if it wasn't for what I have gone through, I wouldn't be who I am today and therefore wouldn't be at a place of peace and feeling how I feel right now. Ironically, I wouldn't be writing this book that hopefully will help many people!

It's the very surreal feeling of appreciation and gratitude of every moment that we have in our life; a feeling that, regardless of how many moments we have left on the planet (because none of us know that) we can choose to enjoy each moment to the fullest. It's a road in which I found acceptance and learned so much about "Jill"; a road in which I am writing and sharing and hoping I may be able to help others as they go through their fears, to set that fear free, and live life to its fullest. It's a road to help people believe in themselves and for them to know that there are many options and choices to make in what they may be going through. If it weren't for "cancer" showing up in my life, I would not be in this moment or place in my world.

On reflection, here is a list of what I believe I have gained along "My Journey" in the last two years:

- **I am happier**
- **I appreciate life so much more**
- **I handle my stress in a much healthier fashion**
- **I live more in the moment**
- **I have learned how to "take care of Jill" beyond any way I had before**
- **I now have learned to love myself**
- **I know I can handle anything that comes my way**
- **I feel more peaceful and calmer**
- **I have more joy in my life**
- **I trust so much more**
- **I surrender to what I can't control**
- **I know I have choices**
- **I take responsibility for my own life**
- **I go out of my way to surround myself with people who are positive and support me in a way that I need to be supported**
- **I am more aware of how important (no, actually critical) my thoughts are**
- **I am not afraid of dying**

All that may seem weird or strange to some people, but that is what I have experienced since getting that dreaded word that many can't even say: cancer. The energy revolving around that word is so negative that I believe it's created such fear in so many people. Most people actually cringe when they hear it.

I'm not so naïve that I don't understand that getting this disease for many people has ended in tragedy. I have lost my mother, my mother-in-law, five close friends (three of them have passed since my diagnosis two years ago) and my beloved dog to this disease. All I'm saying is that I believe that our culture has created so much negative energy around the word that it is no wonder so many people die from it every day. My way is simply a different way to look at it. It doesn't mean my way is right or yours is wrong. It's just a different perspective.

Although this may seem very difficult to understand, I believe that my perspective has gotten me to where I am today. Depending on whom you talk to that has been a part of my journey, the fact that I'm doing so well is still somewhat confusing compared to others with a similar diagnosis. I accept what has come my way with wonder, appreciation and profound gratitude.

As I am writing this book I am at the second year anniversary of getting the news of my diagnosis. Sometimes it feels like it was only a few months ago, and those two years have literally sped by like the speed of light. Other times, it feels like it was light years ago...like another lifetime. Either way, I am grateful and feel blessed that I am still here to share the planet with my family, friends and even the strangers I will be meeting in whatever time I still have left to live.

This is a beautiful poem sent to me by my friend Barb when I was going through a very dark time. It impacted me tremendously:

"My Good Friend Fear"
By Brittany Luise Snedden

Ah, my good friend, fear
I am afraid
Afraid of the full strength of my heart
Afraid of my greatness
Afraid of my darkness and my powerful light
Afraid of loneliness and of surrendering in love
Afraid of inaction, and afraid of regret
Afraid of pain, in all its forms
I ask myself, "What is the antidote for Fear?"
Not Courage, not at first
Wisdom. Wisdom is the antidote
Only in meeting Wisdom can I release my confused friend, Fear
But first there must be quiet
There must be a surrendering, complete and utter humility
A giving up, a giving in, a final letting go
Solitude
Only in this place can the smallest seed then become the Sequoia
All great things began small
First I must see that I am holding Fear's hand
I look up to make eye contact with Fear
A pained smile unfolds
We both know it's time
But it's hard to let go of old friends
I begin to peel my fingers out from between hers
Slowly, gently
I pull my body away
My steps begin to veer to the right
And the space between us grows
As I cross the street to walk with Wisdom instead
And I do look back, before I turn the corner

Jill Robinson

The smallest nod of my head says goodbye
As though I know this is for the best
I turn away, and wisdom takes my hand
My body begins to shiver
I tremble and sob and grieve the loss of my dear friend Fear
Who has kept me company for so long
She knows me so well
But when the sobbing ends, and body becomes quiet for the first time
Wisdom, now embracing me, pulls me up to my feet
And gently lifts my chin
And we walk on, towards her good friend,
Truth.

"Where there is hope, there is life. It fills us with
fresh courage and makes us strong again."

— Anne Frank, The Diary of a Young Girl

Epilogue

Since the beginning of my journey more than two years ago, many people suggested I write a book about the choices I made. It was suggested that I could help others through their own journey by sharing the fact that I embraced both the medical and holistic worlds in cancer treatment. As I mentioned, at first I would laugh and think to myself: *I can't write a book!* However, that's exactly what I did. But the process of writing "Jill's Journey" was indeed a journey on its own...

Soon after I had surgery and I had an epiphany that **"It was time to really move forward with the mindset of a 'survivor' and a healthy person",** I was in an intense healing mode. I wanted to support my body as a healthy person more than I ever had before in my life. As I was resting and healing from the surgery and all that my body had gone through, I had time to think. *Should I write a book? Does that feel like it would be in my highest good? Would it help people with their own journey if I did? Do I have the energy for that?* These were all questions that ran through my mind. Whenever I meditated on the thought, I would envision writing the book in a warm place. I would get a vision of a beach, the sun, and palm trees. I could feel the warmth of the sunshine. I could feel a sense of quiet.

I shared this with a few people, and in the end it was my husband, Steve, that encouraged me to go away to my favourite beach on the planet – Siesta Key, Florida. His thought was that there was no better place to repair and heal from all I had been through than a place that was dear to my heart. My doctor supported the idea as well. It sounded like a great thought, but I wasn't totally convinced. I had been through almost two years of being so dependent. It was indeed a rough road. The thought of going away on my own was intimidating, but also appealing.

I decided to look into the idea. I truly believe that if something is meant to be, it falls into place with very little effort. That's exactly what happened. I found a place in Siesta Key, Florida where I stayed back in 2007. Weirdly enough, it was the first place to pop up in the search. It was available for four weeks at a phenomenal rate. The flight was cheap. It was a familiar place where I knew my way around and there were people there to help me should I require it. I shared my findings with Steve and he encouraged me to book it. With nervous trepidation, I did just that.

The day soon arrived and it was time to go. It was a blur. I was trying to find the balance between getting ready and resting. I was still repairing and had moments of being exhausted. I have a clear memory of sitting on the plane and looking out the window as the rest of the passengers were boarding. As the plane started to back up, I suddenly felt a sense of panic. *What am I doing? Am I crazy? I've depended on so many people for so long! What if I can't handle this?* I could feel my heart racing. I honestly felt like I was going to bolt. But then, in less than a minute, I could feel this wave of peace run through me. A thought came to me. *You're going to be okay, Jill. You NEED to do this. You will be taken care of.* I also thought: *what is the worst case scenario? If you can't handle it, you can just come home.* It was a defining moment for me. I settled into the plane ride to sunny Florida. The preparation for this trip and the flight had knocked the wind out of me. This is something I would never have even thought about in the past. It had much more of an impact than I thought it would have.

In the first few days, I was in bed most of the time. I had caught a cold bug and just felt exhausted. After those days, I slowly started to feel better. I decided to start to write. I stared at the blank, white screen. The flashing cursor was almost taunting me. *Where do I begin?* I had brought my journals with me. I had talked to my friend Herb (my editor) a long time before I even accepted moving forward with writing the book. He said way back then, "Just write Jill…just write down your thoughts as they come to you. We can clean it up and move it around as we go." So I did just that, I started writing. I referred to my journals and just kept writing. I would take breaks taking short walks on the beach. I would rest and honour my body. I would meditate. I would sleep. I was healing…

The process of re-reading my journals proved more difficult than I had anticipated.

As I went through the notes in my journals, I had very difficult moments. It was like I was reliving everything. It was like I was going through the emotions of the journey yet again. Two weeks into my healing time, I felt like I had enough. *This is too much. I don't want to read this stuff, never mind write about it! Why am I doing this? Who is really going to care about this information anyways?* Had I been at home, I most likely would have pushed the writing aside. I would have tried to find a million excuses to avoid writing.

I talked to Steve and Simone that night. They both said pretty much the same thing. "Breathe Jill. Remember you are there to heal. Healing happens on every level. This book needs to be written…if not for other people, for yourself and your own healing journey." Their words rang true. I continued to type away, rest, meditate, heal, write, rest…

After four weeks, I felt so different. I had written most of what

I wanted to share about my journey. I felt rested, relieved, and peaceful but, I was missing my family and friends. I was missing my holistic practitioners.

I continued writing here and there after I returned home. The rest… is history. It feels surreal, but wonderful.

I know writing "Jill's Journey" has been another opportunity for me to heal on yet another level. As a result, it will hopefully contribute towards the healing of others. My profound gratitude for all the "gifts" that have shown up in my life…which includes family, friends, practitioners, strangers, and yes…even cancer.

Acknowledgements

Where do I begin? The gratitude and humbleness I feel towards all the family, friends and total strangers along my journey feels… overwhelming. The kindness, support, care, and love I have received from so many people was quite literally…awe-inspiring.

First of all, I would like to thank Herb Holst, my friend and editor, for keeping me on track and keeping me sane through the different stages of writing Jill's Journey. Your diligence, insight, support and hard work, to make this book actually happen, is so appreciated. If it wasn't for you, I believe the book would never be completed!

My gratitude for each of the holistic practitioners that helped me in many ways through my journey is beyond words. I feel blessed that I had so many complimentary healers at my fingertips. If I hadn't embraced the holistic world through my twenty year old business, it would have been a completely different story. It's because of these incredible people that I designed the book to not just share my journey to wellness, but also be used as a reference and resource to help people along their own journey from a holistic perspective.

Thanks to each of the hospitals, doctors, nurses and technicians for all the medical support through my difficult journey and "unusual" case. We are living in a very exciting time in which technology keeps on changing to help humans live longer. Each of these people attended many years of schooling to help their patients the best way they know how – through medicine. They all were very genuine in wanting their patients to get better through the medical "tool pouch" of suggestions. I believe we are fortunate to live in a time where we have this type of technology to support us through different situations of our wellness needs, from the medical model.

Thank you to the pre-reader volunteers – my cousin Debbie, Simone, Sandi, Fran, Connie, Jen, Andrea, Trudy, Deborah and Wendy - for agreeing to be the important part of giving feedback and suggestions once the book was almost ready to go. Your commitment to being honest and true in how you felt about the book and the edits was so wonderfully inspiring. It's because of each of you that the final edition of the book felt so "complete" to me.

My love and gratitude goes to each of these people who supported me in so many ways that I would have to write another book just about that! It is incredible to me how your true friends come to the frontline when you need them the most. Thank you to:

- Andrea for your beautiful energy, smile and support
- Ann for your endless caring and beautiful treatments of Shiatsu
- Al and Wendy for many years of friendship and support
- Austie, Lexi, Ollie and Boo for bringing sunshine into dark days with your sweet love for your Auntie Jilly
- Barb, for being that solid rock, inspiration and sounding board when I needed it most
- Bev for your delightful sense of humour and novella texts that brighten my days
- Carol for your incredible gift of intuition and the glow of warmth you gift to so many
- Cherry for making my brother so happy and me so happy as a beautiful, caring friend
- Cheryl for your solid friendship, Reiki and beautiful caring energy
- Cindy for your love and support and making me giggle

- Connie for your guidance and suggestions to make the book a reality and for your beautiful, sunny spirit
- Dave for your incredible help with ideas and support on the publishing process, and for your amazing treatments
- Debbie for being the most incredible cousin in the Universe – our "sisterly" love for each other is both humbling and inspiring
- Diana for making me smile and for constantly checking in on me
- Dr. C. for "getting to the bottom of things" and finding new ways to help your patients
- Dr. D. for supporting my journey for so many years
- Dr's. H. and J. for helping me with Traditional Chinese Medicine
- Dr. R. for being so open, loving and supportive of me and my decisions
- Dr. S. for your warm smile and being so incredible at your job
- Fran for your love and support and making me giggle
- Gayle and Bruce for the beautiful cards and flowers when I needed them most
- Heather and Janel for your undying efforts and friendship
- Jason for saying those never-forgotten words – "you got this, girl"
- Jen for being one of the first people in the beginning and teaching me that "no one else can heal Jill, but Jill"
- Joanne for your wise words and amazing reflexology treatments
- Karen and Craig for your love and for making us so many delicious meals when I was too weak to even get out of bed
- Karen and Randy for a longtime friendship and being so concerned and caring
- Katie for the yummy food you made me when I was in Toronto and I was not enjoying the food offered there!
- Kimmy for your grounded, wise ways and a deep connection that has lasted more than a quarter of a century!

- Krista and Little Prince (and their sweet little girls) for being a solid rock through many difficult times
- Lesley for getting me out of that bed and helping me face the journey…head on
- Lisbeth for your strength and being so determined on the mission to "get Jill better"
- Margaret for your loving Reiki treatments and grounded, solid love
- Maureen for teaching me so much about intestinal health and keeping well
- Melissa for being such an incredible, beautiful healer and friend, and a most extraordinary Naturopath
- Mike and Metka for being so concerned and for grounding me with your long time friendship
- Ron for caring so deeply and looking after me "behind the scenes"
- Sandi for your constant support with making the book happen, making me laugh at your emails and texts, and for being the "photographer extraordinaire"
- Sarah for having us over so many times for dinner and for how loving and incredible you are
- Shar for your beautiful, infectious laugh and constant concern
- Simone for your hours of support, guidance and love through this unbelievable journey - your endless patience, phone calls, suggestions, connections, feedback and help (with not only my two year journey, but on the incredible process of writing this book) is so very much appreciated beyond anything I can say. I can't imagine where I would be in this journey had I not seen your ad "glowing" in that horse magazine many years ago!
- Sue for your many awesome, delightful treatments and your determination and love
- W.T. for your diligent and beautiful advice and support while I was undergoing radiation treatments

- My U.K. family whose love and support makes my heart sing.
- The beautiful friends at the financial institution I worked at - your love, support and unconditional care for me is humbling
- To all the strangers that came forth to help me in many different ways during the fundraisers.

A heartfelt gratitude goes to my Dad for your endless care, love, devotion, driving so many miles, working endlessly on our house, the beautiful flowers (that Steve said were from my boyfriend!) and non-stop support in so many ways. You are so generous on so many levels. Your unconditional, undying love for me is breath taking. You make a daughter very proud of her daddy, indeed.

Humble gratitude to my Mom, who I miss every day; who survived almost 20 years with her own journey through cancer - she taught me about positivity beyond any human I have ever met.

My sweet little brother (or should I say "big" brother!?)... thank you for being the bestest brother in the entire Universe! You bring so much laughter and joy to so many people. Your undying commitment to family not only impresses me beyond words, but I find it awe-inspiring. Those long drives back and forth during my journey solidified to me how important family really is, and it brought me even closer to you, which I didn't realize was even possible. Thank you for your huge heart, your deep generosity, and for just being you.

Proud, warm gratitude to each of my kids for all they have done for me; for their love and support through my ups and downs and through the darkest hours of my life. Brad for making so many people laugh; Chelsea for our incredible talks, your wisdom and your loving concern; Alyssa for your sweet caring ways and our long, deep (very inspiring!) talks; Ryan for looking after and walking PT so many times when I just simply couldn't, and for being such a deeply caring person; Mitch for constantly making me laugh and smile even when I really, really didn't want to; and Lindsey for keeping me company when I was bed-ridden (and even when I was not), making me smile and for your warm hugs when I need them the most.

I want to thank my "amazing husband" Steve. There are absolutely no words that can describe the immense love and gratitude I have for you. During my darkest hours, you were there for me...without judgment and with unconditional love. You care for me and support me far more than anyone can imagine or for that matter, will ever know. Where some spouses would run and hide, you came through like a knight in shining armour to help your "true love" on every level. I am humbled by how loving, caring and thoughtful you are... I feel blessed to be your wife.

I would be remiss if I didn't thank my three beautiful friends that were taken with cancer during the two years I was on my journey. Nicky: I miss your beautiful smile, your infectious laugh and how caring you were to every person you met. Tracy: I miss our deep, profound and intense talks. I miss talking about how you and I were going to change the world by "marrying" the medical and holistic worlds together. I hope that you are looking down and that, at some level, I am making you as proud of me as I am of you. René: I miss the fun we had, our longtime friendship, our fun times with our family gatherings, our talks about "the good ol' days". I miss your witty sense of humour and our funny stories about being in our twenties. I know you are hiking and dancing and having a blast from where you are now.

Finally, thank you to my readers. I appreciate your support and allowing my journey to help you through your own journey...

Love and Blessings,
Jill

Definitions

Holistic Therapies/Treatments/Modalities That I Chose During "My Journey" (in alphabetical order)

Affirmations:

According to the website FreeAffirmations.org, the definition of "Positive Affirmations" is: "Statements which affirm something to be true. This definition is still a little ambiguous so to elaborate, basically positive affirmations, what most people mean by them are **positive phrases which you repeat to yourself which describe how you want to be.** The theory (we believe it is much more than just a theory!) is that when you first start saying your positive affirmations, they may not be true, but with repetition they sink into your subconscious mind, you really start to believe them, and eventually they become your reality, **they become a self fulfilling prophecy and actually become true.** Over time they overwrite any limiting or negative beliefs you may have about yourself or about not being able to do something, and replace them with positive thoughts and beliefs which instill confidence, belief, positivity, ambition and much more".

Applied Kinesiology (AK):

"Applied Kinesiology (AK) is a system of evaluating physical structure, biochemistry and mental-emotional well-being or dysfunction/imbalance within the individual. AK was developed in the early 1960's by Dr. George Goodheart, the hallmark of which is the manual muscle test (MMT).

At the time of Dr. Goodheart's insights, muscle function was understood to be diminished by interference in nerve supply (paresis) or atrophy from disuse, trauma or local disease. Dr. Goodheart observed that a muscle's ability to meet the demands of a manual muscle test could be diminished by much more; inappropriate proprioception, related spinal or extremity joint dysfunction, specific biochemical imbalances, related organ/glandular dysfunction and situational life stress."

Dr. John Millett B.Sc.,D.C
Advantage Chiropractic and Massage
59 Dunsmure Road
Hamilton, Ontario
(905) 547-5393
akchiro@bellbet.ca
www.akchiro.ca

Axiatonal Re-Alignment:

"Axiatonal re-alignment is a therapeutic treatment that re-establishes a connection to our Oversoul, using the acupuncture meridians that are aligned with spin points (energy points/vortices of light to help regulate the cells in our body). During an Axiatonal Re-Alignment these spin points are opened up to increase the vibration and frequency allowing the body to release illness from the body to promote light into the cell for cellular regeneration."

Sarah Harper De Medeiros
www.soulpurification.com

Body Memory Recall (BMR):

"When a person has been through a life trauma, accident or a significant experience within their life, they can hold on to the cellular memory of the event. This can lead to muscle and tissue guarding, tight muscles, imbalances in the body and much more. By using touch and support, a Body Memory Recall (BMR) practitioner can guide a client through various movements and stretches to help release the affected area and the memory associated with a particular event or trauma."

Sarah Harper De Medeiros
www.soulpurification.com

Bowen:

"The Bowen technique is a dynamic system of muscle and connective tissue therapy that is revolutionizing health care worldwide. For more than 40 years it has been used successfully to treat thousands of people suffering from a variety of illnesses. Developed by the late Tom Bowen in Geelong, Australia, it is often referred to as the 'homeopathy of bodywork', as it utilizes small and measured inputs into the body which stimulate the body to heal itself, often profoundly. The gentle moves on soft tissue stimulate physiological changes and energy flow, empowering the body's own resources to heal itself. The Bowen technique is safe to use on anyone from neonates to the aged and produces lasting relief from pain or discomfort and a myriad of other conditions. Orthodox and alternative therapists have been generous in their praise of this technique."

Melissa Howe, RN., ND., Doctor of Naturopathic Medicine
www.whitepinesclinic.ca

"Bowen is a gentle bodywork technique, positively affecting the client as a whole, physically, emotionally and mentally during the 45-60 minutes session. Bowen Therapy results in a balancing of the body on the structural and functional level, influencing the individual's overall well-being. The therapist applies a specifically located series of gentle movements across the body. The movements are made over a muscle, tendon or nerve and a release of the tension vibrates through to the nerve within the area rebalancing the body. Clients often feel a sense of deep relaxation following a session."

Simone Usselman-Tod
(905) 746-6797
www.wildaboutwellness.ca; simone@wildaboutwellness.ca

Chiropractic:

"Chiropractic is a branch of the healing arts specializing in the correction of biomechanical disorders involving nerves, joints and muscles. Chiropractors use spinal manipulative therapy (an adjustment) as their primary tool to normalize joint function that in turn helps to reverse disease processes. Most people think chiropractors treat only neck and back problems, however chiropractic therapy often has profound and far reaching effects on an individual's overall health and well-being. This is because the nervous system coordinates and controls all bodily activity, and the chiropractic adjustment optimizes nerve function."

Dr. David Tysdale, D.C.
Dundas Street Chiropractic
(905) 690-1224
www.waterdownchiropractic.com

Coffee Enemas:

"Coffee Enemas are introduced into the colon to heal the body of toxins related to chemicals absorbed into our bodies through our food, prescribed drugs and also recreational drugs. It also helps to detoxify the liver and the colon. Drinking coffee has some of the same effects as the coffee enema. It is a diuretic and can help with constipation. The enema washes out the colon, removing toxic substances, and often nests of parasites, bacteria, yeast colonies, and other debris.

Enemas also stimulate the colon slightly by dilating it a little. It also increases peristalsis and causes the colon to become active, emptying its contents more completely.

Repeated enemas, especially accompanied by colon massage, helps remove impacted feces and food residues, which is common. Certain food items, especially white, refined flour, can turn hard in the colon and stick to its walls."

Maureen McLaughlin, AHC
114 Elmwood Road
Oakville, ON L6K 2A7
Tel: 905-849-1100
Cell: 289-838-5676
www.ahc-oakville.com
www.facebook.com/ahc4health

Colon Hydrotherapy:

"Colon Hydrotherapy, also known as "Colonic" or "Colon Lavage", is a safe, effective method for cleansing the colon of waste material by repeated, gentle flushing with water. The colon was meant to be a sewage system, but by neglect and abuse, it becomes a stagnant cesspool. When it is clean and normal, we are well and happy. Bowel management is an undiscussed topic in our culture today; it's not nice to talk about it. Somewhere there is an unspoken assumption that the bowel will take care of itself. Researchers have shown that regular use of refined carbohydrates and lack of dietary fibre decreases the transit time of bowel wastes and stimulates the production of putrefactive bacteria in the bowel. These factors have been linked not only to bowel diseases such as colitis, diverticulitis and cancer, but also to chronic disease elsewhere in the body. We do not always eat as we should, so we need to know how to clean ourselves out. A good high fibre diet along with a series of colonics (colon hydrotherapy) is the answer. A clean, healthy colon is the key to optimal health."

Maureen McLaughlin, AHC
114 Elmwood Road
Oakville, ON L6K 2A7
Tel: 905-849-1100
Cell: 289-838-5676
www.ahc-oakville.com
www.facebook.com/ahc4health

Correactology®:

"It has been said that: 'Excellence is to do a common thing in an uncommon way'. Correactology® does a common thing - help the body recover from pain, malfunction and disease but in an innovative, uncommon way.

Correactology® is a cellular based system of health care focused on trying to help the body restore a specific directionality to the body's cellular energy. This is achieved by a two-fold testing system and by applying a calculated hands-on stimulus to a specific cellular level on the patient's body. Once the cellular energy is properly directed, the body can attempt to initiate its natural restorative process.

The philosophy of Correactology® is that the body corrects and ultimately attempts to direct its cellular energy along a specific linear path. When the human body undergoes a physical, emotional, or toxic shock, its cellular energy flow becomes altered. This results in a shortage of cellular energy to one or many of the body›s cellular levels. When a cellular level becomes deficient in energy, it loses the ability to do work, resulting in the loss of structure and/or function associated to the affected level."

www.correactology.com

CranioSacral Therapy:

"CranioSacral Therapy is a very light hands-on body work technique that can alleviate stress, pain and dysfunction, by releasing the tissue and compression within the body and improving the function of the central nervous system. CranioSacral Therapy effectively complements your body's natural healing process, and has been known to help alleviate a wide variety of conditions."

Simone Usselman-Tod
(905) 746-6797
www.wildaboutwellness.ca; simone@wildaboutwellness.ca

Dynamic Visioning:

"Dynamic Visioning is a fast and powerful technique that kick-starts the process of shifting old, restrictive beliefs, and catapults clients to a whole new plane of understanding. Self-doubt is 'kicked to the curb' and excitement is felt as insurmountable barriers dissolve.

Many clients experience extraordinary success using the infinite resources and powerful energy of the theta brain wave."

Simone Usselman-Tod
(905) 746-6797
www.dynamicvisioning.com

Essential Oils:

"An essential oil is that aromatic, volatile liquid that is within many shrubs, flowers, trees, roots, bushes and seeds. It is usually extracted through steam distillation. Essential oils are highly concentrated and very potent because of the distillation process. Essential oils have been used for over 3000 years as medicine. They were only rediscovered in the late 18th and early 19th centuries.

Essential Oils do not pose a health hazard nor do they interact with any other modality negatively. For example, a *pure* Lavender Oil can help to heal many kinds of burns. If immediately applied topically, Lavender Oil will stop the pain instantly and can heal the burn without resulting scars. Another example is Peppermint Oil - it can eliminate a headache if applied topically to the back of the neck. All pure Essential Oils have a place in everyone's medicine cabinet."

Cheryl Mahon
905-632-8074

Far Infrared Mat:

A Far Infrared Mat is an electric heating pad (mat) that uses far infrared rays to warm the body. The heat from a Far Infrared Mat penetrates deeper than a typical heating pad: 2-8 inches depending on the model. It is used in thermotherapy. Tip: look for one that blocks the EMF's (electromagnetic frequency from electrical devices).

Herbal Medicine:

"Herbal Medicine is the traditional medicinal practice based on the use of plants and plant extracts. Herbal Medicine is also known as botanical medicine, herbalism and phytotherapy, among others. Many plants synthesize substances that have profoundly beneficial and healing effects and help with a multitude of illnesses that man faces. Even the herbs and spices that we use to season our food yield useful medicinal compounds."

Melissa Howe, RN., ND., Doctor of Naturopathic Medicine
www.whitepinesclinic.ca

Homeopathy:

"Homeopathy (Homeopathic Medicine) is the use of very small amounts of substances (plant, animal or mineral), either alone or in combination in order to support the body in returning to health. It is based on the work of Samuel Hahnemann in the 18th century. He based his medicine on 'the law of similars'", which states that - the same substance which causes illness in healthy individuals, cures it in ill people when used in dilution. For example, poison ivy (*Rhus toxicodendron*): once exposed, a specific set of symptoms develop – in this case an extremely itchy, blistering rash with great restlessness. Yet, this same substance in homeopathic dilution, when given to a person with a similar rash, either from poison ivy, chicken pox, eczema, or likewise, will ameliorate/treat the rash.

- Homeopathics work on physical, mental, emotional and spiritual levels
- There is very little risk of side effects or adverse reactions
- Excellent for children due to ease of administration and vitality to respond quickly

- Many indications for first aid care, as well as the treatment of chronic conditions."

Melissa Howe, RN., ND., Doctor of Naturopathic Medicine
www.whitepinesclinic.ca

Ho'Oponopono:

Ho'Oponopono is a Hawaiian System that was mentioned in Joe Vitale's and Ihaleakala Hew Len, PhD's book: Zero Limits: The Secret Hawaiian System For Wealth, Health, Peace & More. "Simply put, ho'oponopono means, 'to make right' or 'to rectify an error.' *Ho'o* means 'cause' in Hawaiian and *ponopono* means 'perfection'. According to the ancient Hawaiians, error arises from thoughts that are tainted by painful memories from the past. Ho'oponopono offers a way to release the energy of the painful thoughts, or errors, which cause imbalance and disease. In short, ho'oponopono is simply a problem-solving process. But it's done entirely *within* yourself." (Page 42)

www.hooponopono.org and www.zerolimits.info

Ion Cleanse:

"The Ion Cleanse is a relaxing, gentle and effective way of releasing cellular toxicity and allowing your body's natural ability to create and improve health.

This system allows you to eliminate toxins while stimulating circulation and relieving pain. The benefits of the Ion Cleanse differ from person to person.

Why would you detoxify? On a daily basis we are now exposed to chemicals, toxins and pollutants in our food, medications, water and the air we breathe. They are absorbed into your skin (largest organ), digestive system and through your lungs. As this all accumulates, your body systems become more stressed and congested, making it more challenging for your innate healing ability to heal disease and rebalance into 'health'."

Sue Malley
www.everwoodwellness@gmail.com
(905) 627-7381

Infared Saunas:

"Infrared saunas operate at lower temperatures than traditional European saunas with hot rocks and steam. Infrared means "below red" so the elements never get red-hot. The heat is gentle and welcoming, instead of being overly intense. Medical grade infrared saunas utilize ceramic heating elements to gently but effectively heat the skin and trigger a sweat without raising your core body temperature. The result is the most profuse and detoxifying sweat you can possibly achieve, while breathing normally. Canadian researchers have shown that human sweat contains ten times more heavy metals than urine, which means it is the most effective way to detoxify our bodies. The same researchers have also found significant traces of plastic in human sweat. These cancer causing particles can be removed daily in our sweat and prevent a wide range of chronic illnesses that are caused by environmental toxins."

www. Saunaray. Com
info@saunaray.com

Integrated Energy Therapy:

"Integrated Energy Therapy (IET) is another form of energy work, working to the cellular level, to help facilitate a person to release emotion, illness, pain, trauma through various hand positions. An IET practitioner will help the release of energy the person is carrying either physically, mentally, emotionally or spiritually. Once this energy is released and cleared, there is space within and around the body that is open to receive positive energy (Universal Energy). Balance is created."

Sarah Harper De Medeiros
www.soulpurification.com

Iridology:

Iridology is a safe, non-invasive skill that allows us to view the insides of living beings. It is the study of viewing the coloured portion of the eye (the iris), to determine the condition of the fibers. Fibers are the thread-like tissues that compose the structures of the body. Unlike any other analytical tool, Iridology can pinpoint an organ, limb, or a system of the body and give great detail as to the condition of the fibers and the effect that they have on the body. An Iridologist can even tell if healing is taking place.

The purpose of Iridology is to locate rotted tissues in order to remove them through detoxification, then rebuild healthy new tissues through wholesome living habits. In Iridology there are no disease names, only four stages to disease: acute, sub-acute, chronic, and degenerative. These four stages of tissue disease can be viewed through colour or depth. Each trauma to the body removes layers to the front of the iris or causes discolouration. Iridology is an amazing science that can prevent us from entering the later stages of disease, by providing us with the opportunity to change our living habits.

Many people have completely recovered from illnesses with the help of an Iridologist, who can give them concrete directions to change their lifestyle.

Tanya Roerick
Certified Iridologist, Herbalist, Digestive Care Advisor,
Reiki Master and Spiritual Life Consultant
tanyavdesigns@gmail.com

John of God Healing Crystal Bed:

"The John of God Healing Crystal bed is a spiritual treatment device that was channeled through John of God in Brazil. The client lies on a massage table fully clothed under the clear quartz crystals that are suspended 12 inches above their seven main chakra points. Coloured light beams pulse energy through the Chakras to clear any blockages and to align their energies. This works on all levels - spiritually, mentally and physically. While the body receives the energy, the benevolent spirits of the Casa de Dom Inacio are able to use this as a portal to work on the client on a deeper level.

People will feel all different sensations while on the bed from tingling, lightness, heaviness, hot or cold. A feeling of peace and happiness are typical while under the crystals. Others can feel the Entities working on them as the physical healing is taking place. During this treatment, your awareness is heightened beyond your physical body."

Kathy Policelli
Oakville, Ontario
(416) 806-2837
kathypolicelli@Hotmail.com

Kundalini Reiki™:

"Kundalini Reiki™ is "coiled power. It refers to an energy that affects the body, an unconscious, instinctive force that lies at the base of the spine. Kundalini awakens the coiled serpent that remains dormant at the base of the spine until activated. Once awakened and activated, this Kundalini energy is able to move through the body thereby embodying the creative and healing power of the universe.

Kundalini Reiki™ is another lineage of Reiki energy to help promote balance within and around the body."

Kundalini Reiki™ Canada
Kerri Fargo and Karen Fanas
www.kundalinireiki.ca
Sarah Harper De Medeiros
www.soulpurification.com

Lymphatic Drainage Massage:

"Lymphatic Drainage Massage is a gentle technique that stimulates the lymphatic system and encourages the flow of lymphatic fluid, enabling the body to remove toxins and cellular waste more effectively. Lymphatic massage may be used to decrease swelling due to injury, disease or post surgical procedures."

Simone Usselman-Tod
(905) 746-6797
www.wildaboutwellness.ca; simone@wildaboutwellness.ca

Massage:

"Massage is hands-on bodywork addressing muscles, connective tissue, fascia and more, with the effect of increasing circulation, releasing tension and pain and naturally supporting the body to function optimally."

Simone Usselman-Tod
(905) 746-6797
www.wildaboutwellness.ca; simone@wildaboutwellness.ca

Meditation:

As quoted from Yoga International (www.yogainternational.com):

"The Real Meaning of Meditation – What is meditation? How does it work? Can meditation help you achieve genuine peace and happiness in today's hectic often chaotic world?

Meditation is a word that has come to be used loosely and inaccurately in the modern world. That is why there is so much confusion about how to practice it. Some people use the word *meditate* when they mean thinking or contemplating; others use it to refer to daydreaming or fantasizing. However, meditation (dhyana) is not any of these.

Meditation is a precise technique for resting the mind and attaining a state of consciousness that is totally different from the normal waking state. It is the means for fathoming all the levels of ourselves and finally experiencing the center of consciousness within. Meditation is not a part of any religion; it is a science, which means that the process of meditation follows a particular order, has definite principles, and produces results that can be verified.

In meditation, the mind is clear, relaxed, and inwardly focused. When you meditate, you are fully awake and alert, but your mind is not focused on the external world or on the events taking place around you. Meditation requires an inner state that is still and on-pointed so that the mind becomes silent. When the mind is silent and no longer distracts you, meditation deepens." Swami Rama. (www.yogainternational.com)

As mentioned, there are many different types of meditation to choose from. Often times, I will do the type of meditation as mention in my book, which is sitting or laying still and listening to (or tracking) my breath. Here are two examples of "guided" meditations I do on a regular basis as well:

1. Lesley Hannell's Meditation CDs: "Meditation – Beginner", "Meditation – Advanced", "Meditation – Chakra"

Lesley Hannell, M.A., Certified Psychologist - #5708
Phone: (905) 518-8283
Fax: (289) 239-8996
www.lesleyhannell.com

2. Gloria Messenger's "Healing Hands Meditation"

Gloria Messenger
gloria@gloriamessenger.com
www.theangelmessenger.com

Mindfulness Meditation:

"There are many different ways to meditate as the various meditation traditions exemplify, from mindfulness to the use of mantras, movement, dance, voice, breathing, imagery and prayer. Mindfulness meditation focuses on a particular training of our capacity for attention, combined with a very specific attitude.

Rather than living under the spell of an attention that on autopilot goes wherever circumstances call it to go (called exogenous attention), we train ourselves to harness a very different kind of attention that originates in a different part of the brain and is not under the control of circumstances, but under the control of our intention (called endogenous attention). We thus learn to intentionally aim and sustain our attention on a chosen focus, holding all our experiences in awareness without doing anything about them and without reacting to anything that arises in our awareness as we pay attention that way. In addition, we also learn to meet all our experiences with equanimity, or to use an acronym created by Dr. Daniel Siegel, with

COAL, standing for Curiosity, Openness and Acceptance, which is tantamount to Love. This way of paying attention automatically grounds us in the present moment in a non-judgmental way.

The part of the brain responsible for endogenous attention with equanimity or COAL is the medial prefrontal cortex (MPC). It is only found in humans, is the seat of all the organismic functions responsible for physical, psychological and spiritual health, and as the center of our capacity to be aware of being aware, it is the main regulator of our energy flow."

Dr. Stéphane Treyvaud
Phone: (905) 338-1386
Fax: (905) 338-2717
e-mail: info@mindful.ca
website: www.mindful.ca

Myofascial Release™:

"Myofascial Release™ is an effective, whole body approach of hands-on treatment, by a skilled professional, where sustained gentle pressure into myofascial restrictions is used to eliminate pain and restore motion. John Barnes is a pioneer in the field and is an amazingly skilled therapist, teacher and mentor. The fascial system acts as a fiber optic, capable of carrying enormous amounts of information at incomprehensible speeds to the over 50 trillion cells of our body.

Fascia is a strong connective tissue which spreads throughout the whole body. It is an uninterrupted three-dimensional web that interpenetrates every structure of our body. Trauma or inflammation can cause a binding down of the fascial web, causing pressure and pain on nerves, blood vessels, organs, muscles and bones that cannot be picked up on regular medical tests. John F. Barnes Myofascial Release™ is an effective, whole body approach of hands-on treatment, by a skilled professional, where sustained gentle pressure into myofascial restrictions is used to eliminate pain and restore motion."

Christine Grant Physical Therapist, BScPT, John F. Barnes
Myofascial Release™ Practitioner, Reiki Master Teacher
Oakville, Ontario
yourinfinitewellbeing@gmail.com

Naturopathic Medicine:

"Naturopathic Medicine is a multidisciplinary holistic approach to health care. It is both an art and a science, which blends centuries old safe and effective therapies that are in harmony with the planet and your body, with current advances in science and the study of health covering all aspects of family health; from prenatal to geriatric care for the body, mind and spirit. Naturopathic Medicine is:

- A primary form of health care
- Alternative and complementary to conventional/allopathic medicine
- A holistic and coordinated approach to health care
- The diagnosis, treatment and prevention of dis-ease
- The treatment of the causes of illnesses, not the suppression of symptoms and customized treatment plans
- Based on 'the healing power of nature' ('vis medicatrix naturae' Latin)
- Supportive of each individual in their return to a natural state of balance
- The integration of several natural therapies with long histories of efficacy
- Individuals taking an active role in the treatment and maintenance of their health
- The understanding and effective application of Clinical Nutrition, Homeopathic Medicine, Herbal Medicine, Lifestyle and Individual Counselling, Traditional Chinese Medicine,

Massage Techniques, & Hydrotherapy as a foundation for acute, chronic, preventative and long term health care."

Melissa Howe, RN., ND., Doctor of Naturopathic Medicine
www.whitepinesclinic.ca

Neuro-Emotional Technique (NET):

"Neuro-Emotional Technique (NET) is a mind-body therapy used with great success in alleviating both physical and behavioural conditions, by finding and releasing inappropriate neurophysiological responses linked to unresolved emotional events or situations. It was developed by Dr. Scott Walker D.C. in the 1980's arising from his expertise in Applied Kinesiology (AK) and Traditional Chinese Medicine (TCM).

AK is a system of evaluating physical structure, biochemistry and mental-emotional well-being or dysfunction/imbalance within the individual. AK was developed in the early 1960's by Dr. George Goodheart, the hallmark of which is the manual muscle test (MMT).

At the time of Dr. Goodheart's insights, muscle function was understood to be diminished by interference in nerve supply (paresis) or atrophy from disuse, trauma or local disease. Dr. Goodheart observed that a muscle's ability to meet the demands of a manual muscle test could be diminished by much more; inappropriate proprioception, related spinal or extremity joint dysfunction, specific biochemical imbalances, related organ/glandular dysfunction and situational life stress.

Of importance in NET was Dr. Goodheart's correlation of meridians of acupuncture with his muscle-organ relationship. In NET, the meridian-emotion correlates of TCM are applied; lung-grief, liver-anger, kidney-fear, as examples.

So NET uses the MMT to establish the existence of a neural

emotional complex or NEC. An NEC results from a normal emotional response to an event, situation or person not being extinguished (as in Pavlovian Conditioning). The NEC likely forms if an organ system or tissue is under duress at the time, or the stimulus is overwhelming.

In the 1890's, Ivan Pavlov was studying salivation in dogs when he observed, upon just entering the lab, the dogs would begin to salivate. This frustrated his studies but from this observation he developed his theory of the Conditioned Response, where any organism can develop a physiological response to a stimulus associated to an event, given sufficient intensity and repetition of that stimulus linked to the action. Pavlov found the conditioned response is "extinguished" by repeating the stimulus without the event or action that followed previously.

The neurophysiology of the emotional response can best be understood by Dr. Candace Pert's discovery of the "opiate receptor" in the 1970s. Communication within the body occurs with the release of "information substances", a category to which neuropeptides belong. Neuropeptides are released as part of our everyday experience. They travel to remote sites in the body, attached to receptors present on every cell in the body and activate the tissues associated. This produces the physiological response to the felt emotion, from a solitary tear to the heart palpitations of a high stress or anxious event. Pretty much any physiological response in the body, appropriate or not, can become associated to an emotion.

NET is a very patient-friendly technique, applied within the time frame of a typical AK Chiropractic appointment. To find out more about NET, supporting research or a practitioner near you, visit www.netmindbody.com."

Dr. John Millett B.Sc.,D.C
Advantage Chiropractic and Massage
59 Dunsmure Road
Hamilton, Ontario
(905) 547-5393
akchiro@bellbet.ca
www.akchiro.ca

Osteopathy:

"Traditional Osteopathy is a natural medicine which aims to restore function in the body by treating the causes of the pain and imbalance. To achieve this goal, the practitioner relies on the quality and finesse of their palpation and works with the position, mobility, and quality of the tissues."

Norm Hatch, Osteopathic Manual Practitioner
Rockhaven Massage Therapy & Osteopathy
www.rockhaventherapy.ca
(289) 895-8181

Psych-K:

Psych-K is an energy balancing technique that allows one to "identify and correct" disempowering subconscious beliefs. When the subconscious has new positive beliefs programmed in replacing the old disempowering ones, one's reality will start to manifest that which supports the new desired positive belief. The problems in dealing with the subconscious are that no one knows how to deal with it. They don't know what is in there, or how it works. They don't know how to access it. And they have limited to no tools to make positive changes. Psych-K does all of that very effectively.

Psychotherapy:

"The practice of psychotherapy is the assessment and treatment of cognitive, emotional or behavioural disturbances by psychotherapeutic means, delivered through a therapeutic relationship based primarily on verbal or non-verbal communication."

Lesley Hannell, M.A., Certified Psychologist - #5708
Phone: (905) 518-8283
Fax: (289) 239-8996
www.lesleyhannell.com

Reiki:

Reiki is a natural, complimentary therapy that is effective in encouraging the holistic healing of many difficulties. Reiki promotes the healing of many forms of injury and physical injury and even can address the healing and release of emotional or mental issues. It is a modality that can be used in harmony with (but not replacing) medical intervention and other allopathic options. Reiki can thus lead to health and harmony. Reiki is a powerful tool toward individual spiritual growth and can even lead towards improving your own intuitiveness. Clients have shared the following benefits: less stressed, more relaxed, more awareness, more clear, more balanced, less or no pain, better sleep, etc.

Reflexology:

Reflexology is an ancient/natural healing art based on the principle that every part, organ and gland corresponds to areas on the feet. By applying specific pressure to these "reflex" points, peripheral nerves in the feet send a message to the Central Nervous System to adjust tension levels throughout the body. The sympathetic nervous system, which is responsible for the "fight-or-flight" response, gives way to the parasympathetic system, which is responsible for the rest, repair and healing response. More simply stated, by applying specific pressure to these "reflex" points, reflexology can decrease stress/tension, improve circulation (lymphatic, blood), and improve the natural healing function of the body.

Shaman:

"Traditionally, the term Shaman referred to one within aboriginal communities who was a healer and visionary. The Shaman worked with the physical and spiritual, or energy body, of a person to help clear blockages within the Light Body often related to past traumas and manifesting as illness."

Lesley Hannell, M.A., Certified Psychologist - #5708
Phone: (905) 518-8283
Fax: (289) 239-8996
www.lesleyhannell.com

Shiatsu:

"Shiatsu is a Japanese massage therapy based on Chinese medicine, which has been practiced for thousands of years. Shiatsu has more in common with acupuncture than with traditional massage and is sometimes referred to as 'acupuncture without needles'.

When one's body is in a state of good health and balance, the chi is traveling unimpeded through all the meridians. However the chi can get blocked very easily, for a wide variety of reasons as diverse as one's diet, activities, emotional state, the weather, or any physical or emotional trauma. When the chi is blocked, we experience symptoms of discomfort, pain or emotional upset. Even tumours are considered manifestations of blocked energy flow over a very long period of time.

'Shiatsu' means 'thumb pressure' in Japanese. The shiatsu therapist uses their thumbs to work along all the meridians in the body to find where energy is blocked and releases it with the appropriate amount of pressure. The chi can then flow smoothly through the channels and the body can start to heal itself. The patient should feel a lessening of symptoms and a greater sense of peace and well-being. Since its purpose is to restore harmony to the energy flows of the body, shiatsu can treat a wide variety of conditions. Headaches, back and neck pain, PMS, fatigue, and depression are all quite common conditions and there are so many more that respond well to shiatsu."

Ann Crawford, Certified Shiatsu Therapist
Dundas Street Chiropractic
(905) 690-1224
www.waterdownchiropractic.com

Spiritual Messenger:

"A Spiritual Messenger is someone who chooses to listen to the spiritual guidance available to all of us on this human journey. They have usually had a Near Death Experience and/or an Angel Visitation and truly know and want to share that there is guidance available for everyone. Their mission intention is to assist others to hear this ALL LOVE messages independent of whether others are receptive or not. They are someone who has found the JOY of ALL Source Love and is filled to overflowing with its infinite energy."

Gloria Messenger
gloria@gloriamessenger.com
www.theangelmessenger.com

Supplements:

"Supplements are often Vitamins and Minerals either alone or in combination with herbs, homeopathics, and/or glandular, that are created and prescribed in order to supply a deficiency, stimulate or re-balance, reinforce, restore or enhance an individual."

Melissa Howe, RN., ND., Doctor of Naturopathic Medicine
www.whitepinesclinic.ca

The One Command®:

"The One Command® identifies what clients would like to change in their lives, and offers a fast and easy six step process which quickly converts negative thinking into positive. The One Command® shifts old negative thought patterns, focuses on the positive, and accesses theta brain waves, with guided intentions and can create astounding results in health, relationships, finances, purpose and self image."

Simone Usselman-Tod
(905) 746-6797
www.wildaboutwellness.ca
simone@wildaboutwellness.ca

Therapeutic Touch:

Therapeutic Touch is a contemporary interpretation of several ancient healing practices. Contrary to the name, the practitioner does not "touch" the client, but uses his/her hands as a focus for facilitating healing. It is administered with the intent of helping people change their energy in the direction of better health on every level - physical, mental, emotional, spiritual. Therapeutic Touch is practiced by thousands of health care professionals and has been accepted by a number of hospitals in Ontario as a nursing intervention. Scientific research and experience shows Therapeutic Touch can elicit a relaxation response, reduced anxiety, decrease pain, enhancing the body's natural healing process.

ThetaHealing™ Technique:

"The ThetaHealing™ Technique was developed by Vianna Stibal and is a process that releases subconscious programs that are creating challenges in your life. The challenges that may be cleared range from physical, mental, emotional or spiritual. Practitioners are trained how to quickly and easily reach the Theta brainwave to access the beliefs that may be holding any issue in place, through what is known as 'Digging'. They can help discover how those beliefs have served the client and help to quickly let them go. This simple yet powerful technique has changed many diseases and emotional issues into health and well-being."

Kathrine Williams
Master ThetaHealing™ Instructor
Certificate of Science
www.ThetaHealerCanada.com

Traditional Chinese Medicine:

"Traditional Chinese Medicine (TCM) is an ancient form of medicine dating back over 2500 years. It usually includes the use of acupuncture in combination with nutrition and herbal remedies, in order to balance the flow of Qi or Chi (energy) within the individual."

Melissa Howe, RN., ND., Doctor of Naturopathic Medicine
www.whitepinesclinic.ca

Yoga:

"Yoga training allows the individual to step back from the business of life, slow the thoughts of the mind thereby becoming less reactive to situations, and therefore bringing a sense of preparedness to both mind and body. Yoga practice begins by practicing asana postures with the focus on aligning the spine and the limbs as a means of "waking up" our awareness and strengthening the mind's ability to focus. Cultivating a deeper connection between mind and body harnesses the thoughts of the mind into the present moment and by doing so, the 'monkey mind' becomes still and quiet. With a heightened awareness of the body and a quieter mind, we become less reactive to the challenges we are faced with in our daily lives and therefore better equipped to deal with stressors as they arise. Each time we step on to our mats for practice, we move in to the role of the observer, watching without judgment we therefore begin to see the nature of our behavior and the role that our egos play in attaching to one, or a combination of the kleshas ('kleshas' are the veils that each human mind creates shaping the perception of ourself and our relationship to the world around us). Over time, when we see ourselves and our tendencies clearly and honestly, we then are able to dissolve the kleshas permitting us 'to let go of the past, take no thought of the morrow and live in the eternal present'." (Iyengar 4)

Barb Leese
Yoga Instructor
barbleese@gmail.com
www.YogaAlliance.org

References

Holistic Therapy Practitioners That Helped Me On My Journey (in alphabetical order by first name)

The following is a list of the amazing practitioners I chose to see throughout my healing process. They all are incredible in their field of expertise and were a **profound** part of my journey. I believe each and every one of them had an important, inspirational and significant role to play in my healing. I truly believe that they played as much a part in my personal recovery as the practitioners of conventional medicine.

Ann Crawford

Specialty: Certified Shiatsu Therapist

Bio: Ann Crawford, Certified Shiatsu Therapist, graduated from Kikkawa College in Toronto in 1994, one of only two 2200-hour shiatsu training programs offered in Canada. Currently in her 21st year of practice, she has studied and integrated several other energy modalities into her treatments. She is passionate about her work, finding it an honour to work with individuals and to be an active participant in her clients' journey towards better health and joy.

Ann is also a certified EdxTM practitioner (Energy Psychology) and a student of animal communication. She also has a B.A. in French and a certificate for Teaching English as a Second Language.

Contact Information:
Ann Crawford
Dundas Street Chiropractic
(905) 690-1224
www.waterdownchiropractic.com

Barb Leese

Specialties: Experienced Yoga Teacher

Bio: Barb has always had a passion for health and mind/body wellness; by age ten she had left home to train professionally with *Canada's National Ballet School* where she went on to graduate with honours. Joining the *National Ballet of Canada* as a classical dancer, Barb performed across Canada, the United States and throughout Europe, performing both classical and contemporary roles. Her next career was in musical theater with the *Phantom of the Opera* performing with both the Toronto and the International touring companies. She became associate director of the Toronto production and was involved with various other musical productions. Currently, at *Sheridan College*, Barb teaches anatomy/physiology and dance technique for the Bachelor of Musical Theatre Performance program and is associate director of the movement program for The Elder Research Centre. With additional certifications in yoga, personal training and mind/body, Barb brings a wealth of knowledge and experience to her teaching, offering classes that balance strength and flexibility in an atmosphere of openness and trust. Over the last five years, Barb has trained many yoga instructors through her 200 hour Yoga Alliance registered Yoga Teacher Training program. Barb's quest for knowledge and her personal mantra that "anything is possible" inspired her to complete her Masters degree in July 2015 at York University studying the effect of yoga on post-secondary dance training.

As a recipient of the Burlington Civic Recognition Award for International Achievements, Barb is delighted to be using all of her experience to assist people in finding personal wellness and performance excellence through the mind/body connection of yoga and dance.

Contact Information:
Barb Leese, MA, Eryt, Rys
barbleese@gmail.com
www.YogaAlliance.org

Carol Shaw Peirson

Specialties: Medical Intuitive; Intuitive Counselor; Energist

Bio: Carol has been a Medical Intuitive, an Intuitive Counselor and an Energist for many years. She employs holistic and spiritual approaches to supporting each individual's innate ability to heal themselves physically, mentally, emotionally, psychologically and spiritually. She works with individuals, families and groups as well as teaching through workshops and seminars. Carol has previously worked as a Nurse Practitioner, Psychotherapist and College Teacher.

Contact Information:
Carol Shaw Peirson
carolshawpeirson@gmail.com

Cheryl Mahon

Specialty: Reiki

Bio: In 1999, at the Academy for Healing Arts in Burlington, Cheryl learned Reiki and was introduced to Essential Oils. She took three more courses in Reiki, Usui, Komyo, Gendai and Karuna. She then became a distributor for Young Living Oils which fits beautifully with Reiki. Diffusing the oils helps to relax clients, purifies the air and gives an overall feeling of wellbeing.

Contact Information:
Cheryl Mahon
(905) 632-8074

Christine Grant

Specialties: Physiotherapist, John F. Barnes Myofascial Release™ Therapist, Reiki Master Teacher

Bio: Christine Grant has been working as a registered physiotherapist for the past 23 years and is passionate about using John F. Barnes Myofascial Release™ to treat patients in her private business. She has experience in a wide range of patient conditions and treatment techniques, having worked for many years in both the hospital and community setting. She has seen incredible results using

Myofascial Release in a wide range of conditions of injury, trauma, pain, neurological conditions and imbalances in the body and melds it with her extensive knowledge of the body and other treatment approaches. Christine is also a Usui Reiki Master Teacher through the lineage of Libby Barnett and loves teaching Reiki as well as incorporating it into her treatments. "Treating using a whole person approach to wellness is very gratifying and I continue to be both humbled and passionate about at the potential results we can achieve together as part of the healing journey."

Contact Information:
Christine Grant, Physiotherapist, BScPT, John F. Barnes
Myofascial Release™ Practitioner, Reiki Master Teacher
Oakville, Ontario
yourinfinitewellbeing@gmail.com

Christine Riedel, High Priestess Selena

Specialties: High Priestess Selena, CRM, CLC, CHT; Shamanic Alchemical Creation High Priestess; Intuitive Prosperity Creation Coach and Healer

Bio: Christine provides services, training, and gatherings for spiritually-aware, mission-motivated women who are ready to move beyond the fear and limitations of their past, return to wholeness, and harness their authentic feminine creative and intuitive power.

Christine also assists Gaia's Intuitive children and their parents in learning how to understand, harness and utilize their special skills and abilities so they can joyfully fulfill their spiritual missions on Mother Earth.

As a fourth generation intuitive, Christine has been talking to animals, Nature, and spirits for as long as she can remember. Her love for all animals and nature led her to train and begin offering Inter-species Consultations and Training on a professional level in 2003. Over ten years later, Christine has been working professionally as an Animal Communicator and Teacher serving clients all over North America and is highly recommended by veterinarians near and far. In 2008 Christine added Shamanic Services and Spiritual and Intuitive Coaching/Consulting for her human clients, after receiving guidance from her Animal and Spirit Guides that happy, healthy, balanced humans equal a happier, healthier environment for all animals. In addition, Christine's personal and spiritual experiences in healing her own abuse trauma and victim mentality make her uniquely qualified to help clients break free from the chains of fear, shame, and self-sabotage.

In April 2015, Christine completed an intensive Alchemical Creation Priestess Process with Lisa Michaels and received her Priestess name, "Priestess Saraswati Of The Unfolding Blue - Keeper Of Wild Wisdom" and in April 2016 completed the intensive Alchemical Creation High Priestess Process receiving her High Priestess name, "High Priestess Selena, Sunshine In The Night Sky, Singer For The Lighted Beings That Dwell In The Deepest Darkness" fulfilling her lifelong dream of deepening her service to the Goddess, Gaia, and the Web of Life as she continues to help strengthen the relationship between people, animals, nature, and the Divine.

Christine's services masterfully assist her clients to access, reclaim, and embody their natural authentic feminine power and the Goddess within. Simultaneously integrating Gaia's creative secrets with their own, Christine's clients master living a rich soul-satisfying life while confidently contributing meaningfully to the world on their own terms.

In her spare time Christine enjoys spending time with her three children and is constantly learning from the family dogs, Shapiro and Violet, and cat Gloria. Although over the last couple of years many of Christine's beloved animal companions, including her horse and teacher Chakra, have passed on, she continues to learn from them, work with them, and help other animals and people with their stories, medicine, and wisdom.

Contact Information:
Christine Riedel, High Priestess Selena
christine@christineriedel.ca
info@gaiamysteries.com
www.gaiamysteries.com
www.christineriedel.ca

Correactology® Health Care Group Inc.

Correactology® Practitioners and Correactology® Center Locations

Members of CHCG Inc. have graduated from the Correactology® Practitioner Program, are certified by the Canadian Association of Correactology® Practitioners and are licensed Correactology® Practitioners running Correactology® Centers who provide alternative health care services called Correactology® Health Care throughout Canada and/or abroad.

Julie Bédard CHCP®; Kirsti Conron CHCP®; Jenny Davidson CHCP®;

Nicole Fredette CHCP®; Luciano Ingriselli CHCP®; Allan LaPointe CHCP®;

Louis LaPointe CHCP®; Michael LaPointe CHCP®; Julie Léger-Dimaio CHCP®; Mathieu Roy CHCP®

(*Thank you to Julie Bédard and Michael LaPointe for helping me at your Oakville Clinic)

Locations:

Barrie, Blind River, Guelph, Milton, Newmarket, Oakville, Rouyn-Norand (Quebec), Sault Ste. Marie, Sturgeon Falls, Sudbury, Timmins and Val Caron.

Contact Information:
For a location nearest you, visit: www.correactology.com

Dr. David Tysdale, D.C.

Specialties: Chiropractic; Author; Filmmaker

Bio: David has taken many paths during his life, including, biological sciences, humanities, pre-hospital emergency medicine, search and rescue, film and media, springboard and tower diving, and Chiropractic. Currently he lives in a small village atop the Niagara escarpment, and divides his time between chiropractic, writing and film making, and enjoying life with his family.

Contact Information:
Dr. David Tysdale, D.C.
Dundas Street Chiropractic
(905) 690-1224
www.waterdownchiropractic.com

Gloria Messenger

Specialties: Artist; Author; Spiritual Messenger

Bio: Gloria is an author of several Angel books, guided meditations, Angel Vision cards and is an Angel portrait artist. She is one of the few to accurately create reflective Angel portraits. Her amazing story of an Angel Visitation and the hidden meaning of her birth name – (Gloria Messenger) elevates our perception of a powerful guided journey here. Gloria's 'special gift' as a Spiritual Messenger opens each of us to personal communication with The ALL / The Angels of The Light.

Contact Information:
Gloria Messenger
gloria@gloriamessenger.com
www.theangelmessenger.com

Jennifer Lyall

Specialties: Spiritual Development Expert; Energy Teacher; Intuition Teacher; Dowsing Ambassador

Bio: Jennifer is a spiritual development expert who teaches clients how to *intuitively* know how to achieve the radiant health, luxurious wealth and delicious relationships their heart desires. She shows you how to easily weave spirituality into everyday life to enjoy more peace, happiness, abundance and magic. Whether you are curious about developing your intuition, discovering energy healing or knowing more about your true self, Jennifer is a kind-hearted teacher and mentor who sees your potential and can help light the way on your journey.

Contact information:
Jennifer Lyall
www.jlyall.com
905-315-1619
love@jlyall.com

Joanne Trumper

Specialties: Certified Holistic Reflexologist; Intuitive Healer; Independent Distributor for NuCerity International

Bio:

Joanne is a holistic wellness practitioner, certified in reflexology, Reiki and touch therapy. She is intuitive by nature and incorporates her intuition into her healing work.

Joanne is a holistic reflexologist, addressing the emotion behind the physical ailment and offering the positive affirmation to change the emotion and let the physical healing begin.

She also teaches and guides people through the power of positive affirmations, and how to use affirmations to change your life and your physical health.

Joanne has great passion for energy work, teaching and practicing every day how energy is everything from our thoughts and words to our actions. Energy forms our experiences and our life and ultimately our health. Joanne also has great passion for anti-aging and loves to share her many tips on slowing the aging process and looking and feeling your best at every age.

Contact Information:
Joanne Trumper
jtrumper11@gmail.com

Dr. John Millett B.Sc., D.C.

Specialties: Professional Applied Kinesiologist, Chiropractor

Bio: After studying Health and Fitness at George Brown College, Toronto and Biology at McMaster University, Hamilton, Dr. Millett graduated from the Canadian Memorial Chiropractic College, Toronto in 1989. His decision to study Chiropractic evolved from his interest in fitness but also from the natural health practices of his mother, Mary and older brother Jeff. Dr. Millett found Chiropractic a good fit, with its care of the frame in both injury and prevention but also by the natural health practices embraced by chiropractors throughout its century long history.

Upon finishing his board exams but before graduation, Dr. Millett travelled to Sri Lanka to study Acupuncture at the Columbo South Hospital with London trained rheumatologist and medical acupuncture pioneer, Professor Sir Anton Jayasuriya. It was a life changing experience.

Of even greater significance for Dr. Millett was his introduction to Applied Kinesiology (AK) in 1991, the beginning of his lifelong study and practice. AK is a system of evaluating physical structure, individual biochemistry and mental-emotional well-being. Early in Dr. Millett's AK training a group of experienced AK chiropractors in southern Ontario met regularly, exchanging insights and innovations in AK. It was such an enriching environment for a young doctor.

Dr. Millett had the good fortune of studying with some of the greats in AK, beginning with Dr. David Leaf, Dr. Wally Schmitt and the founder of AK, Dr. George Goodheart, to name just a few. In the mid 90's Dr. Millett began studying NET when its founder, Dr. Scott Walker came up to Toronto. Over the next several years he travelled to California to continue his studies in NET.

Travelling and studying AK go hand in hand as the technique is now practiced around the world and overseen by the International College of Applied Kinesiology (ICAK). In 2001, Dr. Millett became the representative for Canada in the ICAK and in 2009 became ICAK Treasurer. This meant travelling the world to annual meetings hosted by different chapters, learning AK techniques from chiropractors, osteopaths, medical doctors and dentists from the America's, Europe, Russia, Australia and Korea.

Dr. Millett continues to study AK, bringing innovative or tried and true methods to his patients in a person centric holistic model of care, balancing evidence based standards of care with new understandings of health and its decline, from an AK perspective.

Contact Information:
Dr. John Millett B.Sc.,D.C
Advantage Chiropractic and Massage
59 Dunsmure Road
Hamilton, Ontario
(905) 547-5393
akchiro@bellbet.ca
www.akchiro.ca

Joy Marcotte

Specialty: Lomi Lomi Bodywork

Bio: Joy serves her community by offering Lomi Lomi bodywork. This type of massage allows her clients to clear physical, emotional and energetic blockages in their bodies. Joy was called to learn this ancient Hawaiian healing practice when she asked the universe how she could use her gifts and talents to be of service. She answered the universe's calling and is now a Lomi Lomi practitioner at The Lomi Touch.

Contact information:
Joy Marcotte
The Lomi Touch
kjoymarcotte@gmail.com
www.hearttoheartlomilomi.com

Kathrine Williams

Specialties: ThetaHealing™

Bio: Kathrine has a ThetaHealing™ Certificate of Science and is a Master Instructor. She is currently studying for a joint Honour's degree in Women's Studies and Psychology at Trent University. She is world traveled and walked 1000kms through France and Spain, completing the spiritual pilgrimage named, "The Camino" in 2007. She was certified for ThetaHealing's™ "Intuitive Anatomy" in an international class in Thailand in 2012 and received her ThetaHealing™ Certificate of Science from founder Vianna Stibal in Idaho Falls in 2012. From 2013-15, ThetaHealing™ has taken her to some wonderful places like Altanta Georgia, Bahamas, South Africa, British Columbia, Seattle and Montana.

Contact Information:
Kathrine Williams
Master ThetaHealing™ Instructor
Certificate of Science
(705) 868-2821
www.ThetaHealerCanada.com

Kathy Policelli

Specialties: Body Regeneration Specialist; Reiki; Access Consciousness; Angel communication; Raindrop Therapy (with essential oils)

Bio:

Kathy Policelli is a Body Regeneration Specialist and has been trained in various other modalities from Reiki, Access Consciousness, Angel Communication, Raindrop Therapy (with essential oils) and a few others that connect us to the Universal life force. By removing old belief patterns and blockages, she is able to allow the client's body to move forward with healing on all layers and levels. In connection with this, she incorporates the healing energy of the John of God Crystal Healing Bed.

Kathy also has had the privilege of taking groups to Brazil to experience, first hand, the energy of John of God for many years now. She has seen her life transform and many others after connecting to this energy.

Contact Information:
Kathy Policelli
Oakville, Ontario
(416) 806-2837
kathypolicelli@hotmail.com

Krista L. Campure, B.A, RMT, SBD

Specialties: Registered Massage Therapist; Reiki Practitioner; Birth Doula; Bereavement Doula and Grief Support Worker

Bio: Krista Campure is the owner of Therapeutic Healing and Wellness Centre in Dundas, Ontario. She offers Registered Massage Therapy for deep tissue, relaxation, hot stone, lymphatic drainage, Indian Head

Massage, aromatherapy, pregnancy, motor vehicle accident (MVA) and sports injury massage treatments. Reiki treatments, including Axiatonal Realignment, are offered as well. Recommendations for remedial exercise, stretching and nutrition are also offered at her clinic. She has recently initiated a Canine Massage Therapy branch to her current massage therapy services, to assist animals who are recovering from injury or surgery, or to the aging and elderly dogs who are suffering from joint immobility and pain from arthritis and age, and to those suffering from the pain of cancer and illness.

Krista's Doula Care services encompass prenatal, labour and postpartum support. Her mission is to help women and their families to have a healthy and vibrant pregnancy, an empowering and meaningful labour, and a happy and confident postpartum journey.

The Bereavement Doula Services she provides assist women and families during pregnancy and infant loss, and fatal diagnosis. She offers support and care during a difficult time. As an extension to her bereavement services, she also provides grief support work to those who have lost a loved one at any age and for any stage of grief. You don't have to walk the journey alone. Krista is there for you.

Contact Information:
Krista L. Campure B.A, RMT, SBD
Registered Massage Therapist, Birth Doula and Bereavement
Doula, Reiki Practitioner and Grief Support Worker
Therapeutic Healing and Wellness Centre
(905) 536-4497
www.therapeutichealingandwellness.com

Lesley Hannell, M.A., C.Psych.

Specialties: Psychotherapy; Shamanism

Bio: Lesley is a Registered Psychologist who also has studied and applies many alternative and esoteric traditions, including Energy Psychology, Shamanism, Equine Assisted Psychotherapy, Meditation and Mindfulness, Tai Chi and Yoga. She has been in practice for over 30 years and provides counselling to adolescents, adults, couples and families. She also teaches Meditation and Mindfulness as well as Mindfulness Based Cognitive Behavioural Therapy and Mindfulness Based Stress Reduction. Lesley offers a variety of guided meditation CD's that help people embrace meditation in their lives (as mentioned in the book) and also offers meditation classes.

Contact Information:
Lesley Hannell, M.A., Certified Psychologist - #5708
Phone: (905) 518-8283
Fax: (289) 239-8996
www.lesleyhannell.com

Lisbeth Fregonese

Specialties: Quantum Energy Practitioner; Intuitive Energy Healer; Meditation Facilitator; Founder of the Wholistic Wellness Communities based in Ontario

Bio: Lisbeth is an intuitive energy practitioner who uses many tools that she has learned over the years from various respected teachers. Using her intuition, she has incorporated shamanic practices and accessing different dimension and entities to receive messages and guidance on the energy that she is working with. She works with these energies and entities to help others connect with their own power so that they may FEEL the connection to their own physical, mental, emotional and spiritual Energy Being.

Her passion is Martial Arts and has practiced it for over ten years.

She holds a 2nd degree black belt in Karate Do and a 1st degree black belt in Kobudo and she also thoroughly enjoys Qi Gong and Tai Chi and teaches Meditation bi-weekly as well as many other workshops on Spiritual Evolvement.

Lastly, she is the founder of the Wholistic Wellness Communities based in Ontario. She, along with a large community of holistic practitioners/vendors, has created Expos geared to spreading Natural Health and Wellness.

Contact Information:
Lisbeth Fregonese
Founder: Wholistic Wellness Communities
www.wholisticwellnesscommunities.com
Luminous Energetic Pathways Healing Centre
Quantum Energy Practitioner
Intuitive Energy Healer, Meditation Facilitator
www.luminousenergeticpathways.com

Maria del Carmen Orlandis-Habsburgo, Baroness of Pinopar

Specialty: Spiritual and Ritual coach; Practitioner of Shamanic Lore and of Mediterranean Angel Lore; Facilitator of trance states; Dream interpreter; caster of spells and maker of talismans.

Author: *Five Tibetan Chakra Yogas and the Five Great Elements: Book of Basic Instruction. The Essential Handbook of Angel Lore: Discover the Ancient Mediterranean Secrets to Attract Health, Love and Abundance*

Bio: Maria del Carmen "Carmen" was born in a magic landscape shaped by ancient traditions. Through her family she carries the genetic memories of the royal blood lines of the Grail. She received the mystic lore from her father, and her mother trained her in practical magic popular lore. It has been her personal merit to do the work to understand her talent and develop her skills. Spirit placed on her path extraordinary beings and she had great mentors from many traditions. Her hobbies are science of the mind and neuroplasticity, anthropology, archeology, comparative religions, hypnosis and gardening.

People that need Carmen's assistance also address her as Yaya (grandmother). They are always enchanted by the colourful traditional techniques even if most of the time they can only remember a fraction of what happened. Her method works at many levels including the mysterious ways of the unconscious and the spirit. This manifests in change in a person's circumstances and improvements in their physical existence. Ritual triggers healing mechanisms, reduces stress and fosters well-being and good fortune. They all glow when it is time to go home after our sessions.

Contact Information:
yayamariadelcarmen@gmail.com

Maureen McLaughlin

Specialty: Certified Colon Therapist

Bio: Maureen dreamed of being a doctor from the time she started to dream of growing up. Family, motherhood and life in general kept her from her passion and led her to a successful career in the financial sector instead.

In her power years, Maureen endured a blockage and surgery in her colon as well as a frightening diagnosis of Diabetes. Insisting on taking her personal power back and taking charge of her own personal health, Maureen began to educate herself on the body and healing. Synchronicity and her battle with Diabetes led her to a Colon Therapist. Her first experience with colonic irrigation was so powerful she came out of the session saying "I know what I have to do now. I'm going to be a Colon Therapist. People need this." From that moment on, Maureen's life purpose led her to alternative healing practice and education. Maureen now finds herself enjoying her practice as a Certified Colon Therapist, with Dr. Jason Lee, Naturopathic Doctor at Innermedica in Oakville. Maureen believes in educating the client and helping them take charge of their health and life. Her nurturing nature makes the experience comforting as well as productively healing.

Contact Information:
Maureen McLaughlin, AHC
114 Elmwood Road
Oakville, ON L6K 2A7
Tel: 905-849-1100
Cell: 289-838-5676
www.ahc-oakville.com
www.facebook.com/ahc4health

Melissa Howe, ND

Specialties: Naturopathic Medicine; Advanced Bowen Practitioner

Bio: It is Melissa's goal to understand you and your health care needs. By understanding you, she can then provide appropriate education, support, empowerment, and Naturopathic treatments and Care which will dramatically improve your ability to achieve your optimal physical, mental, emotional and spiritual potential.

With over 25 years in the health care field, Melissa Howe runs her practice based on a deep respect and compassion for each individual's unique experience, and a passion and ability to use both the art and science of naturopathic medicine to help in the best ways possible.

Melissa's career in health care began as a registered nurse. Following extensive experience in labour and delivery, as well as several other areas, Melissa became aware of a conflict between her instincts and what allopathic medicine prescribed. The palliation of symptoms was often the primary focus of treatment, rather than the underlying cause. This typically led to a suppression of symptoms and further complications of the existing or underlying condition as well as a dependence on medications and the system itself long term. This, combined with a handful of her own health issues led her to *The Canadian College of Naturopathic Medicine* (CCNM).

As a patient at the Naturopathic College Clinic, she was treated for severe eczema, allergies, asthma, chronic reoccurring colds and flu's, and fatigue. A short time later, feeling the benefits of Naturopathic treatment, she became a student herself. She graduated from their full time program in 1999, which included over 4,000 hours of classroom training and supervised clinical experience during an extended four year period.

Having completed this internationally accredited and highly acclaimed program, and passing the external Naturopathic Physicians Licensing Examinations and provincial examinations in 1999, Melissa became and continues to be a registered and fully licensed Naturopathic Doctor with the College of Naturopaths of Ontario. She is also a member of The Canadian Association of Naturopathic Doctors, Ontario Association of Naturopathic Doctors (OAND), and a non-practicing member of the College of Nurses of Ontario. She is also a certified Wilsons Temperature Syndrome practitioner for Women's Health and thyroid disorders. Melissa continually enhances her qualifications and understanding in this ever-growing field, through the CCNM and OAND's continuing education programs, The Academy of International Bioenergetic Sciences, The Bowen Institute,

The Bowen Therapy Academy of Australia, L'Académie Internationale des Méthods Thérapeutiques Contemporaines and The International Society of Homotoxicology, to name but a few.

As a Doctor of Naturopathic Medicine, she is trained and licensed in the healing arts and science of: Clinical and Holistic Nutrition, Botanical/ Herbal Medicine, Traditional Chinese Medicine & Acupuncture, Homeopathic Medicine, Naturopathic Massage, Hydrotherapy, and Lifestyle Counseling. Melissa is also trained in multiple additional therapeutic techniques including: The Bowen Technique, Total Body Modification, CranioSacral Therapy, Lymphatic Drainage Therapy, Zero Balancing, Reiki, and Meditation.

Contact Information:
Melissa Howe, Doctor of Naturopathic Medicine
Advanced Bowen Practitioner
White Pines Naturopathic Clinic
246 5th Concession Road East
Waterdown, ON L0R 2H1
(905) 690-6123
www.whitepinesclinic.ca

Norm Hatch

Specialties: Massage Therapy; Athletic Therapies; Osteopathy

Bio: Norm has been working in private clinical practice since 2005. His background includes degrees & diplomas in Kinesiology, Sports Injury Management, Massage Therapy, and Osteopathic Manual Practice. Through his commitment and passion for learning, Norm incorporates a unique approach to injury rehabilitation. His approach combines a variety of tools and philosophies in order to address each individual's needs in a complete and holistic manner.

Contact Information:
Norm Hatch, Osteopathic Manual Practitioner
Rockhaven Massage Therapy & Osteopathy
Waterdown, Ontario
www.rockhaventherapy.ca
(289) 895-8181

Ron Honda

Specialties: Biofeedback Therapy; Energy Healer

Contact Information:
Renew You Holistic Health
www.renewyou.ca
(905) 304-0111

Sarah Harper De Medeiros

Specialties: Massage Therapy; Integrated Energy Therapy; Axiatonal Re-Alignment; Kundalini Reiki™; Body Memory Recall

Bio: Sarah is a Registered Massage Therapist and Usui Reiki Master with over 15 years experience. Her innate ability to connect to her own intuitive guidance has led Sarah to facilitate healing in others, while identifying and removing their energy blockages.

As a certified Integrated Energy Therapist Master-Instructor (Angel Therapy), Axiatonal Re-Alignment and Kundalini Reiki™ Master,

Sarah incorporates energy healing modalities such as Reiki and Massage with intuitive guidance, through mediumship and angel communication, providing a customized experience for every client, promoting physical, emotional and spiritual wellness.

In 2012, Sarah was introduced to Body Memory Recall (BMR), a form of hands on healing that integrates gentle forms of touch, pressure and stretch to release old body memory (and the associated pain, stress and illness). Sarah found this technique very freeing in releasing not only physical pain from her body, but emotional challenges in her life as well.

After overcoming and healing her own struggles, Sarah is passionate about combining her intuition, knowledge and experience to help others find their own inner peace, joy and love.

Contact Information:
Sarah Harper De Medeiros
www.soulpurification.com

Sat Dharam Kaur, N.D.

Specialties: Naturopathic Doctor, Author, Kundalini Yoga teacher

Bio:

Sat Dharam graduated in 1989 from the Canadian College of Naturopathic Medicine with awards in homeopathy and psychology. She holds both B.Sc. and B.A. degrees from the University of Guelph and a diploma in fine art from the Ontario College of Art. Sat Dharam was awarded the "Naturopathic Doctor of the Year" award by the Ontario Association of Naturopathic Doctors in 2000 for her work in breast cancer prevention and environmental education.

Sat Dharam developed the *Healthy Breast Program* in an effort to educate women in naturopathic ways to prevent and treat breast cancer. She has taught the *Healthy Breast Program* to patients internationally since 1996 and lectures annually at The Canadian College of Naturopathic Medicine on breast health.

Sat Dharam's bestselling books include '*A Call to Women, The Complete Natural Medicine Guide to Breast Cancer*', and '*The Complete Natural Medicine Guide to Women's Health*'.

Sat Dharam lives with her husband and family on an off-grid organic farm near Owen Sound, where she also has a busy naturopathic practice.

Contact Information:
Sat Dharam Kaur, N.D.
Trillium Healing Arts, 235 9th St E, Owen Sound, ON. Canada
N4K 1N8
(519) 372-9212
www.satdharamkaur.com; www.mammalive.net
satdharamkaur@gmail.com

Simone Usselman-Tod

Specialties: Personal Mentor; Holistic Business Mentor; Registered Massage Therapist; CranioSacral Therapist; Bowen Therapist; The One Command® Circle Certified Facilitator; Dynamic Visioning Facilitator; ThetaHealing™ Practitioner; Equi-Bow Practitioner & Instructor; Wild about Wellness Events Facilitator

Founder Wild about Wellness Inc. www.wildaboutwellness.ca
Co-Founder of Equi-Bow Canada www.equi-bowcanada.com
Co-Founder of Dynamic Visioning www.dynamicvisioning.com

Bio: Health and wellness for people and animals has always been

Simone's passion. Working in a conventional career in the medical field for 30 years, combined with the experience of working with clients in the field of holistic healing and natural health and wellness since 2004, provides Simone with a unique edge when working with her clients and an understanding of the body's natural ability to heal itself. With a special interest in relationships, anatomy, physiology, behaviour, mindset and learning, Simone's curiosity and interests have strongly influenced her choices in career and life. Her passion for learning and growing has led her on her own journey woven with discovery, excitement and opportunity. She now works as an entrepreneur honouring her own unique talents, gifts and perspectives, authentically doing what she loves every day, and making a difference in the lives of others.

Simone offers to support clients in their own personal journey through experiential and interactive programs, mentoring, bodywork, community groups, events and more. She is excited to help clients move forward in their lives personally and professionally, guiding and supporting them to achieve the results they have been looking for. Simone encourages positive choices and introduces new ideas as her clients discover their strengths, improve their self esteem, experience self confidence and achieve personal goals. Simone's enthusiasm is evident as she continues to create programs to support her clients.

As founder of Wild about Wellness Inc., Simone facilitates Wild about Wellness Events, promoting and supporting holistic health and wellness practitioners and provides health and wellness services for people, pets and animals. www.wildaboutwellness.ca

With her lifelong passion for horses, Simone has co-founded Equi-Bow Canada, and teaches Equi-Bow technique, which is a gentle equine bodywork technique to professionals and horse owners. Equi-Bow Canada provides, promotes and encourages excellence in equine care. www.equi-bowcanada.com

Simone's most recent focus has been on teaching others how to shift their mindset to create the results they desire. Co-founding "Dynamic Visioning" has been an exciting focus, as her clients are able to shift their limiting beliefs, using their own

powerful theta brainwave, and create a life according to their own hopes and dreams. www.dynamicvisioning.com

Simone offers 20-minute free consultations to anyone who would like to know more about the services and support she offers.

Contact Information:
Simone Usselman-Tod
www.wildaboutwellness.ca
simone@wildaboutwellness.ca
(905) 746-6797

Dr. Stéphane Treyvaud, M.D., F.R.C.P. (C), FMH (Switzerland)

Specialty: Psychiatrist, Founder and Director – The Mindfulness Centre "Mindfulness-Based Stress Reduction Programs (MBSRP)"

Bio: For mindfulness to become the determining force in our attitude towards life, we need to practice a purposeful kind of attention that we are not usually accustomed to.

Dr. Treyvaud is an adult, child and adolescent psychiatrist. He is a fellow of the Royal College of Physicians and Surgeons of Canada, of the equivalent college in Switzerland (FMH) and a full member of the Canadian Group Psychotherapy Association.

His main interest lies in working with adults and adolescents both individually and in groups, providing psychodynamic psychotherapy and mindfulness meditation training. He practices and teaches an integrative approach to medicine, mental health and spirituality. He offers mindfulness meditation training through introductory and advanced meditation programs, retreats and individual sessions.

His medical training includes specializations in Mind/Body Medicine, Psychoanalysis, Jungian Psychology, Existential Psychotherapy, Developmental Psychology, Mindfulness-Based Stress Reduction, Interpersonal Neurobiology and Sensorimotor Psychotherapy. With Northrop Frye he studied matters of the imagination and spirituality.

His meditation experience goes back many decades and started in the German Black Forest with the first Westerner to become a Zen master and bring Zen to the West, Karlfried Graf Dürckheim. Later Dr. Treyvaud trained under Jon Kabat-Zinn in Mindfulness-Based Stress Reduction as he incorporated mindfulness training in his psychiatric practice. He further deepened his mindfulness training with Shinzen Young in Vipassana insight meditation and with Helen Duquette in the Vanda Scaravelli tradition of Hatha Yoga. He also trained in Interpersonal Neurobiology with Daniel Siegel at the Mindsight Institute in Los Angeles. With thousands of hours of his own meditation experience spanning more than 40 years Dr. Treyvaud cultivates an active meditation practice of his own as he embodies mindfulness as a way of life.

Dr. Treyvaud has been running a private psychiatric/psychotherapy practice for over 25 years. 15 years ago he founded The Mindfulness Centre in Oakville, which incorporates a stress reduction clinic. He has developed an integrative approach to medicine and mindfulness, encompassing both psychotherapy and meditation. Awareness of the importance of mind/body medicine has spread like wildfire and become quite well established within the medical community. Dr. Treyvaud's referral base has thus grown to include over 800 family physicians, medical specialists, pain clinics, psychotherapists and various institutions across the whole Golden Horseshoe from Niagara

Falls to Belleville, as hundreds of patients have now been trained at the Mindfulness Clinic through regular mindfulness programs. He gives regular lectures, workshops and seminars at various institutions, and has presented yearly workshops across Canada at the annual meeting of the Canadian Group Psychotherapy Association.

Contact Information:
Dr. Stéphane Treyvaud
Phone: (905) 338-1386
Fax: (905) 338-2717
e-mail: info@mindful.ca
website: www.mindful.ca

Sue Malley

Specialties: Owner/Facilitator of Everwood Wellness Retreat & Spa; Reflexology, Bowen Therapist, Holisitic Nutritionist, Reiki Master in Usui/Kundalini

Bio: Sue is a Reflexologist, Bowen Therapist, Holisitic Nutritionist, and Reiki Master in Usui/Kundalini. She offers various other therapies and services as well. She is currently a student of Osteopathy at Canadian Academy of Osteopathy. She loves her work and has been embracing Energy Medicine for fifteen years.

Contact Information:
Sue Malley
www.everwoodwellness@gmail.com
(905) 627-7381

Tanya Roerick

Specialties: Certified Iridologist, Herbalist, Digestive Care Advisor, Reiki Master and Spiritual Life Consultant

Bio: Tanya is a Natural Health Care Practitioner with over 20 years of professional training and experience in the field of holistic health and metaphysics: the mind/body/spirit connection. As an Iridologist, Herbalist, Digestive Care Advisor and Reiki Master she is able to go beyond the norm of healing.

Tanya will draw upon gentle, respectful assessments and spiritual coaching techniques to help you transform negative habits and limiting beliefs into positive self-empowerment, in order to lead a happier and healthier lifestyle.

Contact Information:
Windows to the Soul
Tanya Roerick
Certified Iridologist, Herbalist, Digestive Care Advisor,
Reiki Master and Spiritual Life Consultant
Waterdown, Ontario
tanyavdesigns@gmail.com
(905) 512-9973

Resources

Important First Steps

When we first find out that we have a disease like cancer, we may go through different phases of shock, sadness, hopelessness, anger, disbelief and denial. When we are finally ready to move forward with making choices, our heads can be spinning with all the options that we have available to us.

I would like to point out that the resources listed in this chapter do not apply just to those dealing with cancer. **All** of the resources I have put in this chapter could also help people dealing with different conditions or for those who would like to be healthier – physically, emotionally, mentally and/or spiritually.

All of the resources I have listed in this chapter have somehow impacted and changed my life and made my own personal journey go in a more positive way.

Books

"Ask and You Shall Receive: A Miracle For Steven" – Karen Vincent Zizzo

> *"At the age of seven, Steven, a happy, strong, athletic boy, was given three months to live. This is the personal story of the Zizzo family. It is a story of Faith, Hope, Love, and The Power of Prayer.*
>
> *This story is told exactly as the events unfolded – recalled from every raw emotional moment burned to memory. From the time the nightmare began, the family asked, very publicly, for prayer and was encircled with the love and support of the ripple effect of thousands of prayers. The events of this story are incredible. For some, they are unbelievable, for others unexplainable. For many, it's nothing short of a Miracle."*
>
> *(Taken from the back cover of Ask and You Shall Receive: A Miracle for Steven – Karen Vincent Zizzo)*

Regardless of your spiritual belief or religious background, this book is inspiring and beautifully written. It could change the way you look at things and what you believe in.

"Dying To Be Me" – Anita Moorjani

"Dying to Be me: My Journey From Cancer, to Near Death, to True Healing" by Anita Moorjani was a very powerful book that I read soon after I was diagnosed. This is from the inside of the front cover:

> *"In this truly inspirational memoir, Anita Moorjani relates how, after fighting cancer for almost four years, her body began shutting down – overwhelmed by the malignant cells spreading throughout her system. As*

her organs failed, she entered into an extraordinary near-death experience where she realized her inherent worth…and the actual cause of her disease.

Upon regaining consciousness, Anita found that her condition had improved so rapidly that she was released from the hospital within weeks – without a trace of cancer in her body! Within these pages, Anita recounts stories of her childhood in Hong Kong, her challenge to establish her career and find true love, as well as how she eventually ended up in the hospital bed where she defied all medical knowledge.

As part of a traditional Hindu family residing in a largely Chinese and British society, Anita had been pushed and pulled by cultural and religious customs since she was a little girl. After years of struggling to forge her own path while trying to meet everyone else's expectations, she had the realization, as a result of her epiphany on the other side, that she had the power to heal herself…and that there are miracles in the Universe that she'd never even imagined. In Dying to Be Me, Anita freely shares all she has learned about illness, healing, fear, 'being love', and the true magnificence of each and every human being!"

This book helped me realize that no matter how far down the rabbit hole you go with any disease or condition, there *still is hope*.

<u>"Radical Remission" – Kelly A. Turner, Ph.D.</u>

Author Kelly A. Turner, Ph.D. wrote "Radical Remission – The Nine Key Factors That Can Make a Real Difference – Surviving Cancer Against All Odds". What a life changing book! It helped me take the darkest of hours and feel hope beyond hope. This is the **FIRST**

BOOK I would suggest you read if you, or someone you love, has just found out they have cancer.

The following is on the inside cover of her book:

> *"Dr. Kelly A. Turner is a researcher, lecturer, and consultant in the field of integrative oncology. Her specialized research focus is the Radical Remission of cancer, which is a remission that occurs either in the absence of conventional medicine or after conventional medicine has failed." Turner...*"gives the reader the results of her research on over a thousand cases of Radical Remission – people who have defied a serious or even terminal cancer diagnosis with a complete reversal of the disease.*
>
> *The results of this study, which focused on seventy-five factors, include astounding insights of the nine key factors that Dr. Turner found among nearly every Radical Remission survivor she has studied and an explanation of how the reader can put these practices to work in his or her own life. Every chapter of Radical Remission includes dramatic stories of survivors' journeys back to wellness. The realization that the possibilities for healing are more abundant than we had previously known gives people concrete ways to defy the overwhelming prognosis of terminal cancer.*
>
> *This is a book for those who are in the midst of receiving conventional cancer treatment, who are looking for other options because that treatment has done all that it can, or who seemingly have no options left but still feel that the future holds the possibility of hope. Kelly Turner's Radical Remission shows that it is possible to triumph over cancer, even in situations that seem hopeless.*

Encompassing diet, stress, emotions, spirituality, and other factors that profoundly affect our health and well being, Turner's discussion of how our choices can cause the seemingly miraculous to happen will open your eyes to what is possible when it comes to lasting healing."

Again, this would be one of the first books I would suggest to read right after a person finds out they have cancer. It's an incredible book to help people make choices of what to do next. It helps brings clarity and can help you feel more in control of your options. Whether you have just found out you have cancer, or know someone who has, this book helps bring a ray of hope. It is incredibly well written and is empowering.

"There is a Spiritual Solution to Every Problem" – Dr. Wayne Dyer

"In this inspiring new book, best-selling author Wayne W. Dyer shows us that there is an omnipresent spiritual force right at our fingertips that contains a solution to our problems - from ill health to financial worries to relationship difficulties. Drawing from various spiritual traditions, especially from the prayer of Saint Francis of Assisi, Dyer helps us unplug from the material world and awaken to the divine within.

The first part of the book provides the essential foundation for spiritual problem solving. In these chapters, you'll read the words of Patanjali, a Yogi mystic whose teachings and practices deeply affected Dyer and informed his realization that the spiritual force is everywhere.

The second half, organized around the prayer of Saint Francis of Assisi, contains specific suggestions to help readers put spiritual problem solving into practice. Saint Francis's legacy is one of love, harmony, and service -putting our collective energies towards what we are for instead of

what we are against. Each of these last seven chapters begins with a line from this prayer; Dyer then goes on to offer specific and practical suggestions for applying the teaching to everyday problems. These suggestions include affirmations, writing exercises, guided meditations, and other strategies for putting Saint Francis's words and the wisdom of this book into practice.

Profound and thought provoking, yet filled with pragmatic advice, There is a Spiritual Solution to Every Problem is a book about self-awareness and tapping the healing energy within all of us. As Dyer writes, 'Thinking is the source of problems. Your heart holds the answer to solving them.'"

This is the book version of the six CD set that I mentioned changed my life. I first heard the CD's back in the early 2000's. I have listened to it more than ten times over the years, and each time I hear something new. It is literally a life-altering book/CD set.

"Zero Limits: The Secret Hawaiian System for Wealth, Health, Peace and More" – Joe Vitale and Ihaleakala Hew Len, Ph.D.

"This riveting book can awaken humanity. It reveals the simple power of four phrases to transform your life. You should get ten copies of it – one for you and nine to give away. It's that good."

Debbie Ford, New York Times best selling author of "The Dark Side of the Light Chasers"

"There is real potential for this book to start a movement that will end war, poverty, and the environmental devastation of our beloved planet."

Marc Gitterle, MD www.CardioSecret.com

"This book is like a stick of dynamite, and the moment you start reading, the fuse is lit. It blows away all the complex and confusing success paradigms of the past and reveals a refreshing and clear path to transform your life with just one simple step. Be prepared for a journey that is both challenging and inspiring beyond anything you've imagined."

Craig Perrine, www.MaverickMarketer.com

"Vitale has captured the truth that all great spiritual, scientific, and psychological principles teach at the most fundamental level. Boil it all down to the basics and the keys are quite simple – the answer to all life's challenges is profound love and gratitude. Read this book; it's a reminder of the truth and ability you already possess."

James Arthur Ray, philosopher and bestselling author of Practical Spirituality and the Science of Success

I really enjoyed reading this book. It was over a year into my journey when I found it. It was an easy read and was captivating. It was empowering. To this day I use the simple yet powerful technique that Vitale and Hew Len suggest.

Recommended Video

Colon Hydrotherapy:

https://www.youtube.com/watch?v=0AXHD5H9nEQ*

(*this is an excellent, short video about colon health and how critical a healthy colon is in our overall wellness)

"Colon Hydrotherapy, also known as "Colonic" or "Colon Lavage", is a safe, effective method for cleansing the colon of waste material by repeated, gentle flushing with water. The colon was meant to be a sewage system, but by neglect and abuse, it becomes a stagnant cesspool. When it is clean and normal, we are well and happy. Bowel management is an undiscussed topic in our culture today; it's not nice to talk about it. Somewhere there is an unspoken assumption that the bowel will take care of itself. Researchers have shown that regular use of refined carbohydrates and lack of dietary fibre decreases the transit time of bowel wastes and stimulates the production of putrefactive bacteria in the bowel. These factors have been linked not only to bowel diseases such as colitis, diverticulitis and cancer, but also to chronic disease elsewhere in the body. We do not always eat as we should, so we need to know how to clean ourselves out. A good high fibre diet along with a series of colonics (colon hydrotherapy) is the answer. A clean, healthy colon is the key to optimal health."

Maureen McLaughlin, AHC
114 Elmwood Road
Oakville, ON L6K 2A7
Tel: 905-849-1100
Cell: 289-838-5676
www.ahc-oakville.com
www.facebook.com/ahc4health

Breast Cancer Support: Different Examples of Services

Breast Cancer Support Services:

Breast Cancer Support Services is a non-profit organization dedicated to the support of people affected by cancer, with a focus on breast, ovarian and other gynecologic cancers. Survivors and volunteers are the heart of the organization, providing compassionate support in their warm and inviting home and throughout the community.

The programs and services are **free of charge** and are offered with the whole person in mind. Classes and holistic therapies are intended to **support and complement medical treatments** and to encourage spiritual, physical, intellectual and emotional wellness. BCSS services are adapted to the expressed needs of the community and by growing scientific evidence that stress reduction, eating a healthy diet, exercise and a positive support network can substantially improve the health and well-being for people living with cancer and their caregivers.

They provide support, care and information tailored to individual choices and stage in the cancer journey. Their services include:

Peer Support Group: Their support groups enable women with cancer to discover new ways of coping, share experiences, exchange information and resources and become part of a community of care.

Individual Peer Support: This program seeks to match women who are newly diagnosed with women 12 months post diagnosis who can offer understanding and support having been in a similar situation.

Comfort Kit: BCSS Mastectomy comfort kit contains their signature post-surgery pillow as well as information and helpful products to support you during treatment.

Wigs, Prosthesis and Bras: Thanks to the generosity of local suppliers, retail stores and individuals, they have a selection of new and gently used products at no cost to women in the community.

Holistic Therapies: They offer a variety of therapies and practices that are known to help patients cope with the emotional and physical side effects of cancer diagnosis, treatment and recovery. Their team of professional practitioners provide free Reiki, reflexology, therapeutic touch, massage, post-surgery scar treatment, yoga and guided meditation.

Building on 25 years of supporting women and families affected by breast cancer, BCSS is poised for reinvention and expansion. As a result of stakeholder consultation and research, they have evidenced a need to broaden their services to meet a growing demand for psychosocial support in our community. Many in the communities need help navigating the health care system as well as understanding and accessing the many holistic therapies and wellness programs that may provide comfort and healing. In order to better serve the community, the goal is to transition from an organization that focuses solely on specific cancers to one that offers supportive care, wellness programs, resources and referrals to a much larger population.

For more information:
Breast Cancer Support Services
www.breastcancersupport.org
695 Brant St
Burlington, ON
(905)634-2333
outreach@breastcancersupport.org
www.breastcancersupport.org

Wellspring Cancer Support Centres:

History -

Wellspring was founded in Toronto in 1992 by Anne Armstrong Gibson, who had been diagnosed with non-Hodgkins lymphoma in 1988. Along with all her other fears about treatment, survival and the future of her husband and two young children, Anne experienced something more, an overwhelming sense of isolation. She quickly realized that this was an all-too-common experience among cancer patients, and became determined to fill the void.

With the help and encouragement of some of the leading experts in the field of oncology, Anne worked with family, friends and supporters to establish Wellspring, a non-profit organization offering psychological, emotional, social, spiritual and informational support to individuals and families living with cancer. Anne's vision for Wellspring was to create a Canada-wide network of community-based centres that would provide people with the tools they required to cope with cancer.

How Wellspring Works -

More than 85% of cancer patients experience the non-medical consequences of cancer and its treatment: the fear, anxiety, pain, financial worries, isolation and guilt.

Through one-to-one peer support, group support activities, learned coping skills, rehabilitation programs and much, much more, Wellspring has helped thousands of people take an active role in controlling their cancer experience to improve their quality of life.

Wellspring helps with -

- Stress management
- Health restoration and rehabilitation
- Reduced fear and isolation
- Education and information
- Successful transitions back into the workforce
- Financial advice and management

At Wellspring, the focus is on the person, not the disease. As the leading network of cancer support centres in Canada, Wellspring is a sanctuary of understanding where cancer patients, at any stage in their cancer journey, as well as their family members and caregivers, are welcome to participate in programming that will help them move forward with renewed strength, confidence and hope.

Wellspring's model has been recognized by Health Canada as an outstanding example of organizational excellence in community-based health care.

The Wellspring Approach -

Wellspring charges no fees and receives no government or other core funding. Programs and operations are made possible only through the generosity of donors.

Being part of the compassionate and understanding Wellspring community means having the opportunity to talk with others who have been through cancer, access experts and share knowledge and experience in a warm, safe, encouraging and non-clinical environment. Every person who visits Wellspring is unique. They work with every member to identify resources that meet their particular needs and where they are on their cancer journey.

Led by experienced professionals, including psychologists, physiotherapists, therapists and dietitians, Wellspring's more than 40 programs and services span a comprehensive range of categories, from individual and group support activities to learning coping skills, to expressive arts programs and to practical guidance in areas such as nutrition, financial management and workplace issues. All programming is evidence-based and developed and piloted through the Wellspring Centre of Innovation.

For more information visit: www.wellspring.ca

Wellwood:

Wellwood is a community not-for-profit that provides free supportive care programs and services to those living with a cancer diagnosis or caring for someone with a cancer diagnosis. Wellwood has two locations, both in Hamilton, Ontario. Day and evening programs range from information/navigation to peer support to coping strategies that include movement, creative expression and relaxation.

For more information, call (905) 667-8870 or visit their website www.wellwood.on.ca

Miscellaneous

Knitted Knockers of Canada -

Knitted Knockers of Canada is an organization dedicated to providing special handmade breast prostheses for women who have undergone mastectomies or other procedures to the breast. These soft, comfortable lightweight prostheses are available for FREE. They are knit with love by our wonderful volunteers. Some women find traditional breast prosthetics too expensive, heavy, sweaty and uncomfortable. Also traditional prostheses often cannot be worn for weeks after surgery. Knitted knockers on the other hand are soft, comfortable, and beautiful and when placed in a regular bra they take the shape and feel of a real breast. Knitted knockers can also be used to fill the gap for breasts that are uneven and easily adapted for those going through reconstruction by simply removing some of the stuffing

Funding: they are funded by donations only. The knockers are made by volunteer knitters who buy the yarn themselves. Once made, the knockers are donated to Knitted Knockers Canada for distribution. A dedicated bank account has been created. They do not have charitable status so tax receipts are not available.

Public Awareness: they are currently partnering with The Camisole Project and provide a pair of knitted knockers with each free camisole that is given out. They are also working with local yarn shops to have "knit a knocker" night to enlist more volunteer knitters and to help spread the word. They are also in the process of working with various cancer centers to help spread the word.

Knitted Knockers organizations have spread throughout the United States, Europe, Australia and Canada. While all operate independently, they share ideas without any thought of personal gain. Knitted Knockers Canada has a website (http://www.knittedknockerscanada.

com) that you can visit or please like them on their Facebook page (https://www.facebook.com/knittedknockersofcanada).

Their Expenses: are minimal. Costs are for postage, mailing supplies, and promotional material. There are no paid employees.

Community Support: Their generous supporters include Estelle Yarns who have donated yarn to help their volunteer knitters make these beautiful knockers and Ever Soft Fibers who have donated stuffing to help complete the knockers. They also have local yarn shops that have been very generous in acting as drop off points for finished knockers, and offering discounts on the specific yarn they use. They have also had donations from area businesses to help with mailing costs! Donations can be made to help offset costs by sending a cheque made out to Knitted Knockers of Canada and sent to: 115 Fiddlehead Cres., Waterdown, Ontario, Canada, L0R 2H8

Contact: For further questions you can contact Nancy Thomson at nancy@knittedknockerscanada.com

How to get a Knocker: Anyone who would like to request knockers can go to their website http://www.knittedknockerscanada.com and fill out the request form. They will endeavor to get the request filled within 2 weeks.

Radiation Burn Help -

Although the beginning stages of radiation were quite easy to handle, near the final weeks, the pain and burning was incredibly high and almost unbearable. One of the nurses suggested using the diaper rash cream, Penaten® Cream. It made a huge, significant difference immediately. I was so appreciative of her suggestion.

Wigs -

For many women, hair is an important part of their identity. It says so much about who they are and how they want the world to see them.

Ultimately, when women chose chemotherapy as an option for cancer treatment, they will usually lose their hair. I made the choice to get a wig. I really wanted to look like "myself", especially at major events. I decided to get a wig to wear during the time I had no hair. It took me a while to come to this decision. I didn't want to fall into a trap of caring what other people thought about the way I looked. More importantly, I wanted to stay in my authenticity that means so much to me. Many people who lose hair from chemotherapy treatments decide not to get a wig, but I'm so happy I did. I was referred to "The Wiggery", where the owner, Linda, made me feel so comfortable right away. Her warm, caring and kind personality radiated as soon as I met her. At first, I was very nervous and unsure of the whole procedure. My step daughter, Chelsea, went with me for support and to help me make a decision. We had a blast! We were giggling and laughing in no time at all. I tried on many wigs. With her many years of experience, and her obvious passion for her work, Linda found a wig very quickly that matched my own hair beyond anything I had imagined. When she placed the wig on my head, it looked so much like my "normal" hair. It was uncanny! It made me feel good. Because I'm the type of person that doesn't like to draw attention, I felt better in public with it on. I wore it to Chelsea's wedding. Again, I'm so happy I did! When I look at those pictures a year and a half later, I feel good about my decision. I didn't wear it all the time, but it was really nice to have the choice to do so when it felt right.

"The Wiggery"
Linda White
Burlington, Ontario
lwhite@wiggery.ca
(905) 631-0801

About the Author

Jill Robinson has been a practicing holistic health care practitioner for over 21 years and has assisted hundreds of clients with reflexology, Reiki, therapeutic touch, and meditation techniques. Using "Effective Communication" strategies, Jill also offers workshops and courses that can help clients to gain healthier relationships.

While on her journey, Jill attained her certification as a yoga instructor and now offers yoga and meditation classes and retreats.

A resident in beautiful Greensville, Ontario, Jill enjoys her life with her husband, their six kids in their loving blended family, and PT - her hiking companion who is addicted to squirrels!

May the sun bring you new energy by day.

May the moon softly restore you by night.

May the rain wash away your worries.

May the breeze blow new strength into your being.

May you walk gently through the world and
know its beauty all the days of your life.

— Apache Prayer

Printed in the United States
By Bookmasters